The Blessing of Boundaries

Lauren Bell

By Lauren Bell

2005

The Blessing of Boundaries
by Lauren Bell

Printed in the United States of America

ISBN 1-597811-41-6

www.xulonpress.com

Table of Contents

For my AE Girls with love

Acknowledgements

*T*his book is a beginning, and I know I have much more to learn. My family, who has watched me struggle through the exhaustion and encouraged me during the recovery process, can surely attest to this. I could not have compiled these lessons without their love, support, and candor. Our years of serving the Lord together have been the richest of my life thus far. Who would have guessed that God would set the boundaries for these years so that we lived and worked together for this long? My deepest thanks go to Mom and Dad, my sisters Julianne and Amy, and my brother Adam. "The lines have fallen for me in pleasant places; indeed, I have a beautiful inheritance." (Psalm 16:6)

I'm also grateful for the countless others whose investments in my life have made this book possible. I particularly appreciate the following people who helped bring this message to life:

Paul Settle, thank you for helping to make sure I got my theology straight!

Lars and Elisabeth Gren, thank you for your gracious gifts of encouragement and counsel based on your years of lifestyle ministry.

Bob and Yvonne Welch, Bill Gothard, Bernadine Cantrell, Liz Barnard, Christianna Reed, Jen Ransil, Kim Schmidt and Gina Novotny, thank you for taking time to read drafts of the manuscript and give me helpful insights, suggestions, and affirmation.

The wonderful DTC staff members who have walked through these years by my side, thank you for your friendship and encouragement to never give up.

INTRODUCTION

Defining Boundaries

You hold in your hands a summary of lessons learned thus far in my heart's journey with my Savior, Jesus Christ. The first title I considered was *Gratefully His*, for that phrase aptly states my heart's condition toward Him. My father proposed I entitle the book, *True Confessions of an Overachiever*, as a tribute to my hard-driving nature and perfectionist tendencies. Though I think he meant it as a joke, it probably gives you a better clue as to the need for the lessons compiled here.

After further prayer and consideration, I settled on the title now before you, *The Blessing of Boundaries*. My journey has been one of learning the boundaries, or limitations, God ordained for my life before the beginning of time. Ephesians 2:10 says, "For we are his workmanship, created in Christ Jesus for good works, which God prepared beforehand, that we should walk in them." These preordained good works are the boundaries, or guidelines, for living an effective Christian life. Rather than thinking of them in light of our culture, which bucks and scoffs at any hint of restriction, I am learning to see boundaries as a blessing from God.

Boundaries are a concept, a principle that threads its way through Scripture. God used boundaries to define the universe, separating time from eternity, then matter from space. "In the beginning God created the heavens and the earth." (Genesis 1:1) God also uses boundaries to identify His people: His children are *all but only* those who confess their need of a Savior, accept Christ's payment for their sins, and enter into a covenant relationship with their Creator. The familiar words of Psalm 23 describe in vivid analogy the tender care of the Great Shepherd for those at rest in *His* pasture, those within the boundaries of His love. The testimony of Scripture ends with the words of Jesus, defining the boundaries of His own Being as "Alpha and Omega, the first and the last, the beginning and the end." (Revelation 22:13)

By learning to see boundaries as a practical means for living, God's children can know His design for their lives and flourish within the limitations He sets. *The premise of this book is that the most secure and satisfying place for the believer is within the boundaries God designed from the beginning of time.* These limits are His gift to us, a blessing to enjoy rather than a restriction to ignore, scorn or reject.

I have not always seen boundaries as blessings. I confess I am a doer, one who sees many needs and opportunities and seems driven with an inborn determination to meet them all. Operating for years beyond the limits of my physical, emotional, and spiritual boundaries led, inevitably, to exhaustion. At the lowest point of my fatigue, I was no longer a grateful Christian, delighting in my existence as a daughter of the Most High King. Instead, I chafed at the boundaries of life and wished for death to put an end to the sufferings I experienced even while serving God in "full time Christian ministry."

During those months of despair, a friend encouraged me to study the life of Christ, the quintessential example of one who recognized and understood His reasons for living and the boundaries that defined His ministry. Exploring the Gospels with new interest, I began to see Jesus in *purposeful but limited* ministry. He thoroughly understood the boundaries determined by the counsel of the Godhead before the beginning of time. According to these limitations, He focused His ministry on the Hebrews living in the land of Israel. He did not heal every sick person or change the visible structure of government. Nevertheless, He did all that He came to do. Not one purpose of God was left unfulfilled, and He released His life into the hands of His Father with the statement that still rings through the ages, "It is finished." (John 19:30)

We know God has a specific calling for each of His children. Isaiah 6 describes the way He called and ordained the prophet Isaiah. In Jeremiah 1:5, this prophet records God's personal word to him, "Before I formed you in the womb I knew you, and before you were born I consecrated you; I appointed you a prophet to the nations." Psalm 139:14 – 16 may be the most familiar assurance of God's particular calling for His children. David writes, "I praise you, for I am fearfully and wonderfully made. Wonderful are your works; my soul knows it very well. My frame was not hidden from you, when I was being made in secret, intricately woven in the depths of the earth. Your eyes saw my unformed substance; *in your book were written, every one of them, the days that were formed for me, when as yet there were none of them.*" (emphasis mine)

Throughout Scripture we see God defining the boundaries of the lives of His children, calling them to *do* things for Him, but more importantly, calling them to *be* His own. In Hebrews 11, He praises those who followed Him for the faith that motivated them to pursue Him down the paths He forged for their lives. This has been the challenge for me, learning to be by faith the person God had in mind in eternity rather than focusing all my energies on achieving things for Him. This has required reordering my priorities to reflect those Christ established for His life and ministry. What better pattern exists for structuring my time to best accomplish the eternal purposes of God for my life?

Through my studies, I was challenged to see that Christ made spending time in prayer and fellowship with His Father His number one priority. I am learning that this should be my focus as well. My personal time with God should set the pace and define the priorities for my days so that I too do *all but only* those good works prepared for me before the foundation of the world. By flourishing within the boundaries God established to bless me, ministry becomes a way of life rising effortlessly from the fathomless depths of His love rather than the feeble attempts of the flesh.

Perhaps, like me, you have found yourself weary in well doing, exhausted from attempts to meet every need and be "all things to all people." Burnout is a rampant problem in our culture, and an equally significant issue in the church. I read a study in the Spring 2002 issue of healthsmart today whose author cited this staggering statistic: "It has been estimated that 43 percent of all adults suffer negative health effects directly associated with stress." If almost one out of every two adults suffers some kind of health problem related to the pace and circumstances of life in our day and time, we all know someone who can benefit from learning to reset their boundaries by following Jesus' example for living.

Considering how to approach ministry differently is revolutionizing my life and, with the hope that these thoughts may encourage others, I have endeavored to record them. For the doers out there, please consider this an invitation to rest, not a "how to" list. If, however, you are one who has been content to focus just on the "only" part of what you feel God calling you to do with your life, perhaps you need this reminder that He also wants you to do "all" that He has planned for you. As you journey through these heart thoughts, I pray God will use them to illuminate your boundaries and reassure you of His love. This love is not based on performance but on the unchanging, unsearchable wisdom of His will. "Yea, I have loved thee with an everlasting love: therefore with lovingkindness have I drawn thee." (Jeremiah 31:3, KJV) I am confident you will find the richest blessing of your life as you relax within the boundaries of His arms.

CHAPTER ONE

Boundaries: Blessing or Curse?

"Enter by the narrow gate.
For the gate is wide and the way is easy
that leads to destruction,
and those who enter by it are many.
For the gate is narrow and the way is hard
that leads to life,
and those who find it are few."
Matthew 7:13-14

In the stillness of the dawn, I vaguely hear the soft click of the CD player as the power activates and quiet music fills the room. Groaning, I swing my arm toward the night-stand and grope for the remote control. With a point and click in the general direction of the alarm, I turn the music off and the daily debate begins. I can barely open my eyes and know from experience that efforts to read my Bible and pray will probably fail. "Still," I argue with myself, "Only a lazy person can't get out of bed in the morning, and just the thought of time with the Lord should motivate me to get up quickly and embrace Him, and the new day, with joy."

Joy has been a distant friend for months now as I struggle to face each dawn at all. Getting up is only one of my troubles, for the mental debate carries over to almost everything I try to do. Sometimes I can force cheerful compliance to the demanding schedule and others' expectations, and sometimes my resolve gives way. After years of serving, surrounded on all sides by my mission field, I can no longer count on my ability to paint on a happy face and enjoy the presence of others. More and more, I retreat to my room only to lie on the bed looking up at the ceiling and wondering if I am losing my mind, my Christianity, or both. "How did I get to this place?" I wonder as I slowly swing my legs out of bed, find the floor, and prepare for another full day.

WHEN LIFE GETS OUT OF BOUNDS

As the firstborn in a Christian family, I learned the importance of making God a priority early in my life. At the age of four, my mother led me in prayer and I confessed my sins to God, believed that Jesus died to pay the penalty for my debt, and accepted my place in the covenant family of His grace. Since my father served in the United States Air Force, we moved every few years. At the age of twelve, while we were stationed in Izmir, Turkey, I began to understand with a more adult mind what it meant to follow Christ. One night, after a Bible study, I came home from the lesson weeping as the Holy Spirit convicted me of the part my personal sin played in the crucifixion. With this realization came the desire to give something back to the One who died and rose again on my behalf.

Following this revelation, I purposed to spend time each day reading the Bible and praying. This practice, though sporadic throughout my teenage years, laid an important foundation for me as it introduced me to the possibility of daily interaction with a personal God. Shortly before I turned sixteen, my parents decided I should spend the next summer working overseas with a group of Christian young people. I knew this would require more than the reluctant efforts I put into my weekly chores, so I chose what appeared to be the easiest trip and signed up to travel to England and Scotland with a group whose focus would be evangelism. At that time I had yet to learn that often the most strenuous work is not the physical labor we associate with fatigue at the end of a long day, but rather the consuming demands of mental and spiritual activities.

During my time overseas the family packed up from the small town on the Florida coast where we had lived for three years and moved to a base east of St. Louis. I experienced many anxieties while away from home, but feeling really alone for the first time brought me face to face with the opportunity to learn how to more deeply relate to God as father, confidante, and friend. I reached a crossroads that summer at which I chose to pursue a relationship with God based on what I personally believed of His Word rather than simply following truths I learned from my parents, pastors, and others along the way.

I came home with a new resolve to serve the Lord, determined to give the rest of my life to "full time Christian service." I fully expected that to mean He would send me to Africa to live in a grass hut surrounded by natives, cut off from civilization and all its amenities. So the next year when the brochure for summer mission trips arrived, I pored over the descriptions and settled on a team going to Liberia, West Africa to build a home for missionaries.

After the trip, amidst the fall schedule of choir rehearsals, club meetings, and weekend football games, I began considering options for college. I eventually settled on Messiah, a small Christian liberal arts college located near Harrisburg, Pennsylvania, and decided to major in elementary education thinking that would prepare me to work with children and provide me with skills I could use on any mission field.

The next four years passed quickly as I jumped into classes, developed new friendships, and crammed every extra-curricular activity I could into my schedule. I did not forget the commitment to minister ... I sang in small groups that gave Sunday night concerts at churches in the surrounding area. For two years I served as class chaplain and then, during my senior year, I was elected chaplain for the student government association. I counseled as a resident assistant in a freshman dorm my sophomore and junior years. I buried myself in activity and outreach, but still managed to graduate with honors.

Following graduation, I got a summer job working for the county where my family now lived in Florida and prayed for direction about the next step. A door opened in August when I was invited, along with my sister, to spend some time in Indianapolis working for a Christian organization. As Julianne and I headed north, I believed I was on the verge of realizing my dream of doing important, "full time" service for the Lord. After a few days, I feared a mistake had occurred. I wanted to change the world for God, but my new boundaries consisted of working in the laundry room, washing and folding seemingly endless piles of sheets and towels. However, I did not stay there long, and that fall I had the opportunity to teach in the ministry's school for several weeks before the president asked me to join his office staff. I agreed and spent the remaining weeks until Christmas working in his office, helping with correspondence, getting to know young people from other parts of the ministry, and watching our leader in action. His energy and stamina amazed me! By the time I flew home to spend the holidays with my family, I was exhausted just from trying to keep up with him.

I spent most of the Christmas holiday sick and in bed.

When I returned to Indianapolis in January, my ribs still hurt from bronchitis induced coughing. I lasted about three weeks before the leadership decided to send me home. None of the available positions seemed a good fit for my personality or training, and my energy failed to rebound after the illness. I left with no intention of working with this particular ministry again, but the Lord had other plans. Within the year, I was on an airplane, this time headed for an assignment in Texas.

I jumped right into my responsibilities in Dallas as the assistant to the director of an eight-week program for young ladies called EXCEL. EXCEL stands for Excellence in Character, Education and Leadership and is based on the character and skills outlined in Proverbs 31. I ran the office, helped train new staff members, led music, occasionally counseled and filled in anywhere else a need arose. I felt I had found my niche, a place to serve and to disciple, a calling God gave me during my years as a resident assistant at Messiah.

During the summer of 1995, events were set in motion that signaled a significant change in my life. One day my boss called me into his office to tell me that he and his wife felt the need to shift their attention to other avenues of ministry and intended to begin searching for a replacement. They eventually interviewed my parents for their job, and after much prayer, my father agreed to move the rest of the family to Dallas and assume this new position.

I served as the interim director that fall while the family fulfilled commitments in Florida and prepared to move. The responsibility of caring for the daily needs of almost 100 young women overwhelmed me at times, and some mornings my devotional time consisted of lying facedown on the floor and reciting the words to the hymn "How Firm a Foundation" over and over to myself. "Lord God," I begged, "You promise that 'The soul that on Jesus hath leaned for repose, You will not, You will not desert to his foes. That soul, though all hell shall endeavor to shake, You'll never, no never, no never forsake'."

Prior to the family's move to Dallas, God gave me a vision for developing a discipleship program for EXCEL graduates. After they settled in, my parents gave me the green light to begin developing courses, recruiting other instructors and inviting alumni to attend the five-month discipleship program. In the winter of 1997, the new course called Advanced EXCEL began, and another chapter of life started for me.

Though not on a foreign mission field, during this time I was learning to see "full time ministry" as anything God called me to do that involved loving Him and passing that love on to others. As a little girl, I dreamed of one day becoming a Dallas Cowboy cheerleader. Through Advanced EXCEL, I became a cheerleader with a different calling than professional sports; I motivated young women to set goals and dream of influencing the world for Christ. For me, this still meant constantly *doing*, but the time was quickly approaching when my ability to do would be limited and God would begin redefining His expectations for me.

Before our second anniversary in Dallas, my father was asked to put his years of personnel experience to work by leading the staff at the international headquarters of the ministry. Dad agreed and launched the family into yet another challenge. We maintained our residence and responsibilities in Texas but spent several months of the year meeting additional demands in Illinois. For two years we commuted about every three months. During those months of rushing from one set of responsibilities to another with only sporadic breaks spent sleeping – because who had energy for anything else? – my delight in the Lord and joy in ministry began to wane. A fatigue-induced depression I experienced at times in college resurfaced like an oft-repeated dream that leaves a faint sense of unease hours after rising from sleep.

We could appreciate living in both worlds, but we breathed a collective sigh of relief when God opened the door for us to return to Texas full time in 1999. My responsibilities changed again when my parents took over the running of the hotel that housed our conferences and events in Dallas. I became the event coordinator and jumped into the role with a passion, putting anything and everything I could think of onto the calendar. As we began our fourth year of service together, I should have realized I needed to pace myself for a marathon, but instead I started with a sprint and then found myself in the daunting position of needing to maintain the faster pace.

We made adjustments as we headed into the year 2000, but the damage had already occurred. After years of throwing myself repeatedly against my physical limits, my body started to break down. At first I just noticed an increasing difficulty getting out of bed in the morning that I attributed to spiritual backsliding and waning zeal for the Lord. Surely I suffered from a lack of inner resolve or some other sort of personal failure! Somewhere along the way my daily devotions had become an item on the list, one step on the daily climb that I had to check off in order to deem the day a success.

Along with my struggles with fatigue, I began noticing other problems: headaches that lasted for days and uneasiness in my stomach that never quite went away. Then I began forgetting things, walking half way down the hall from my office only to turn and slowly go back to my desk wondering why I left in the first place. I could no longer do the arithmetic in my checkbook without writing it all down like a grade school student, and I wondered if old age was destined to set in before I turned 30. I grew increasingly anxious and at times wanted to scream and cry over issues I knew should not provoke such strong emotions. I lived in constant fear of an emotional explosion; concerned I would lose control in front of guests or staff members who expected an always-gracious hostess. When I found myself afraid to drive places alone because bridges and overpasses looked too much like an attractive ticket to heaven, I knew it was time to ask for help.

Shortly after making up my mind to seek counsel, we hosted a medical conference at the hotel. A nurse we knew from the Chicago office attended, and I asked her to meet with me. When she walked into my office and sat down, I started talking: listing my physical symptoms, explaining my take on the emotional symptoms and hesitatingly admitting the spiritual ones. To my relief, she agreed that something was definitely wrong. Later that weekend I met with one of the doctors at the conference, and he quickly concurred with the nurse's opinion, ordered a prescription for me, and suggested some additional tests.

I met with another doctor in January and was relieved when he defined my illness, though the title: "Multiple Systemic Exhaustion Syndrome" sounded intimidating. Some might find a diagnosis threatening, but for me, it gave hope. For so long I thought perhaps it was all in my head and I could will myself to feel differently if I just followed the right steps and applied the correct principles in my spiritual walk. Discovering physical realities contributing to, if not causing, my emotional and spiritual pain gave me hope and a tremendous sense of relief.

Since that time, I have required lots of extra rest, many cumulative days, weeks, and months to allow my body to recoup the energy drained by years of pushing myself beyond my boundaries. Think about a rubber band. It can stretch beyond its limits when necessary and hold things together for a time. But, eventually, if pressured long enough, even the toughest rubber band will snap. When my energy finally "snapped," I had to learn to accept my physical limitations and recognize them as God's blessing rather than a curse. For a person accustomed to pushing through any obstacle and rising to any challenge, this has been incredibly humbling. So much of my identity was wrapped up in my "doing," and I did not even realize it.

More than physical benefits accrued during my recovery. Every few months, it seems, the Holy Spirit pulls back a curtain into emotions hidden and ideologies warped during the frenetic pace of the last few years. With each revelation into my soul, I have a choice: to walk forward into the freedom He offers or to retreat into the comfort of old patterns that led me down a wrong path. At times, I have felt like a piece of meat on the tenderizing block as the Lord showed me false paradigms I believed and sins I ignored. I resisted recognizing them as much as, if not more than, the physical limitations because I so wanted to do things for God and to be a person who made Him proud. Losing the ability to *do* forced me to reevaluate what gave me worth and to learn to see myself accurately from God's perspective. Carolyn Custis James has observed, "...that life's struggles are the shortest route to a deep appreciation of our need to know God better," and I have found this to be true. (When Life and Beliefs Collide, p.22)

DISCOVERING THE PRINCIPLE OF BOUNDARIES

At one particularly low point in the emotional struggle with my new reality, a friend suggested I look at how Jesus approached His ministry and develop a paradigm for ministry based on His life. I had many ideas of what "full time ministry" entailed, but perhaps the reason for my illness was that I was missing the points Christ emphasized by His example. For instance, He did not hurry. He was never anxious. He did not do, do, do all the time. He spent a great deal of time walking and fishing and talking with his friends, not things I would put on a list of "things most important to do today for God" – or for myself – for that matter. Yet, as he struggled for breath on the cross, Christ said, "It is finished."

And, in 33 short years, he completed the task God set before Him and changed the course of eternity.

You see Jesus understood the principle of boundaries. He designed them, and wove them throughout the fabric of Scripture. In Genesis 1:1 we learn, "In the beginning God created the heavens and the earth." He created and separated these two entities, limiting them one from the other with established boundaries. In verse three, God calls forth light and then divides it in verse four from darkness. He set limits right from the beginning: heaven and earth, light and darkness, day and night.

Creation continued until God had fashioned each part of nature to His specifications. Then, in Genesis 2:8 we read, "And the Lord God planted a garden in Eden, in the east, and there he put the man whom he had formed." The garden itself had boundaries, and God gave Adam and Eve careful instructions regarding their limits within this utopia. "And the Lord God commanded the man, saying, 'You may surely eat of every tree of the garden, but of the tree of the knowledge of good and evil you shall not eat, for in the day that you eat of it you shall surely die'." (Genesis 2:16-17)

We know what happened, of course. Adam and Eve disobeyed God and ignored the boundaries He designed for their protection. And so they established the pattern for mankind: God gives us limitations for our good and, viewing them as a curse rather than a blessing, we manipulate, reset, or outright reject them. Abraham and Sarah would not wait for the promised heir, but instead stepped outside of the bounds of God's direction. Almost daily the news reports remind us of the consequences still reverberating through the Middle East as the descendents of Ishmael and Isaac continue the family feud begun thousands of years ago. Moses went beyond God's instruction and struck the rock twice, bringing forth water for the thirsty Israelites, and forfeiting his opportunity to set foot in the Promised Land.

King David insisted upon counting his fighting men despite counsel to the contrary, and his sin brought devastating consequences to an entire nation. A careful reading of Scripture reveals countless illustrations of the problems that arise when we follow our fleshly inclinations to overstep the boundaries God has established for our good. Praise Him, as we read, we also witness the sovereign hand of God working out His eternal plan for the good of His people through failures as well as triumphs.

Jesus was the only Man who ever lived without violating the boundaries of righteous, holy living. Not only did He fulfill the entire Law of God, but by putting on the robe of human flesh, He accepted the boundaries of humanity by His very presence on the earth. He taught the disciples in John 4:34, "My food is to do the will of him who sent me and to accomplish his work." "It is finished," He gasped as He hung dying on the cross. (John 19:30) So, in life and in death, He accomplished the full will of God. How could He do this? He knew the Father's will. This will established the boundaries of His life, the ways in which He spent His time, energy and what few possessions He had.

Jesus entered heaven to the timpani of triumph because He disciplined Himself to do *all*, but *only*, what the Father designed Him to do in this life. Therefore, He is the best one to teach us how to recognize the boundaries God designs, not just for Mankind, but also for our individual life callings. Each one of us benefits when we follow Christ's example. The doers learn to accept those "limitations" designed to save them from themselves; they learn to do *only*. And the complacent or timid learn to flourish by pursuing more than they think they could possibly do; they discover they can do *all*.

FAITH, PRAYER, AND BOUNDARIES

Christians are motivated by a variety of things, some spiritual, most selfish. Some demonstrate their faith by what they do, while others are content to sit on the sidelines watching unless specifically prodded into action. Some habitually push the limits of their boundaries, while others consistently reshape them, making them smaller and seemingly, more manageable. I will develop this concept further in a later chapter, but for a moment let's think together about one of the key measurements of a person's faith: his prayer life. Imagine if you will a continuum that symbolizes the span of the Christian life.

On the far left are those who do not pray, or if they perform a ritual they call prayer, it is shallow and affects little change in their lives or the lives of others. They do not involve themselves much in the work of the church or in relationships with other people. Their boundaries include *only* themselves and their interests, and though they warm the pews on Sunday, little zeal for Christ warms their hearts throughout the week. These believers may even use boundaries as an excuse: "I can't do that ... it's outside my boundaries. I'm not called to work with children, youth, the elderly, etc." While claiming to be living within their boundaries, this lack of service may be a visible manifestation of an inner issue of selfishness, fear, or pride.

On the far right are those who also pray little, but rather than solely concentrating on their own interests, they pour themselves into doing good works. They have little time for prayer because they are too busy doing *all* the work they can. They neglect their Heavenly Father's admonition in Psalm 46:10 to "be still and know that I am God." They forget that God has a specific work for us to do, but we only accomplish it effectively by working within the boundaries of His ways, His timing, and His strength. Anything done in our way, timing, and strength is iniquity. These believers often mix the freedom and joy of Christian life with a perfectionistic, performance-driven mindset, and eventually work themselves to exhaustion. Proverbs 14:12 warns us,

"There is a way that seems right to a man, but its end is the way to death." Compulsive, driven "service" may well be an outward indication of an inner lack of faith in God to accomplish His will.

The balance and perfect example of course, is Christ Himself. We would find Him in the center of our imaginary continuum. He focused on prayer and spent large amounts of time with His Father. Though surrounded by needs and obviously the most competent, not to mention, anointed, one to meet them, He did *all but only* that which the Father willed. In this matter He showed tremendous restraint, and provided us with an important example, one that I over-looked for years.

God's richest gifts lie within carefully crafted boundaries, boundaries He designed as a blessing, not a curse. He longs for us to find them and flourish there. In my zeal to do things for God, I took my focus off of Him and became consumed with my own works. I was doing good things: encouraging families, discipling young ladies, teaching, singing, organiz-ing, leading. But my eyes were filled with the needs and my time consumed with trying to figure out ways to meet them rather than looking to God to meet them. You see, somewhere along the path of life, I assumed responsibilities never designed to rest on my shoulders. Christ never allowed the needs around Him to overwhelm Him because He kept His focus on the Father. He did what God instructed and trusted Him to multiply limited efforts to meet never-ending needs.

When I became too busy about "the Lord's business" to stop and pray, much less wait, trust, love, and obey as He commands, I was bound to suffer consequences. Busyness on the one hand, and inactivity on the other, betrays a lack of faith, which results from a lack of prayer and meditation upon the words and character of God. I realize now that, while faith without works is dead, works without faith were leading me just as surely toward death. Let me explain.

The spiritual roots of working in my own strength and bypassing daily direction from the Father are pride and a lack of trust. I see the overwhelming needs around me, both nearby and throughout the world, and it seems that God is not in control. Surely, if He were paying attention, He would not allow all the suffering and sorrow reported daily in the news. My solution: try to make up for His apparent lack of attention through my own efforts. Perhaps He really does want me to be the "General Manager of the Universe!"

This sentiment directly contradicts Jesus' command in Matthew 11:28-30, "Come to me, all who labor and are heavy laden, and I will give you rest. Take my yoke upon you, and learn from me, for I am gentle and lowly in heart, and you will find rest for your souls. For my yoke is easy, and my burden is light." A correct understanding of this text alone could have spared me from the consequences of working outside my boundaries. In my zeal for the works and impatience with God, I forgot the important truth that I, a mere vapor, never supply something God lacks. He always supplies what lacks in me. My efforts to supply what I supposed God lacked were leading me toward spiritual death. I still cannot pinpoint the moment in which my faith and love were overcome by works and pride, but it happened and the results devastated me.

The emotional result of this misguided spiritual effort was thinking, "Not only is God not handling these problems, no one else seems to be doing a good job of fixing them either. Therefore, it is up to me to save the world!" In a warped way, this seemed noble: to courageously take up the standard and tackle formidable obstacles. But, in reality, this mindset is pure, unadulterated pride, an affront to God and offensive to others. Jesus summarized the Old Testament commandments by instructing His own to love God with their entire being and to love others as themselves. Pride makes obedience to this command impossible. I cannot love

God if I do not trust Him, and I cannot love others if I do not see them as partners in the tasks of life God lays before us.

BALANCE WITHIN BOUNDARIES

As I have reflected from my sickbed, I now understand the answer is to humble myself and accept that God has not asked me to do everything alone. Christ Himself has already accomplished the most important things in all eternity, and therefore, it is not up to my feeble mind, will, and flesh to finish anything. God graciously calls His people to take part in His continuing work of redemption, but we must get the marching orders from time spent at His feet, not outline them for ourselves and set off on our way without Him. Assuming responsibility for the sorrows of the world will overwhelm our emotions and lead to depression and the death of joy, hope, faith, love … the very things that should characterize the Christian life.

I have already mentioned some of the physical results I experienced from following faulty paradigms about God, His work in the world, and my own ability to meet needs. The boundaries are as real as gravity. My body was bound to shut down under the weight of the unrealistic demands I placed on it, just as surely as it would fall if I stepped off the roof of a 10-story building. And I know I am not alone. One does not have to look far to see other well-intentioned Christians struggling with physical illness, emotional burnout, and the spiritual side effects of doing too much.

Jesus admonished His followers, "Enter by the narrow gate. For the gate is wide and the way is easy that leads to destruction, and those who enter by it are many. For the gate is narrow and the way is hard that leads to life, and those who find it are few." (Matthew 7:13-14) Most of the time, this verse makes us think of unbelievers, and that is the obvious application. However, I believe my experience illustrates an application for the Christian as well. There is a way to "minister" which is broad and includes using the methods and mentality of our culture to accomplish God's goals. This usually leads to iniquity: doing the work in my own strength rather than God's. Rare is the person who follows Christ's example and limits herself to her understanding of God's will for each particular situation. Yet, I would suggest that this is the "narrow way" for the one who truly desires to follow in the footsteps of Christ and extend His kingdom. In the narrow way lies the blessing found only within God-ordered boundaries.

The apostles certainly experienced this as they journeyed around their world spreading the gospel. Acts 16:6-10 gives one description of how they were led to preach specifically within the boundaries of God's will. "And they went through the region of Phrygia and Galatia, having been forbidden by the Holy Spirit to speak the word in Asia. And when they had come up to Mysia, they attempted to go into Bithynia, but the Spirit of Jesus did not allow them. So, passing by Mysia, they went down to Troas. And a vision appeared to Paul in the night: a man of Macedonia was standing there, urging him and saying, 'Come over to Macedonia and help us.' And when Paul had seen the vision, immediately we sought to go on into Macedonia, concluding that God had called us to preach the gospel to them." The apostles' ministry was purposeful, but it was also limited by the sovereignty of God's plan for His glory, their good, and the extension of His kingdom. Our challenge, like theirs, is to do *all* the will of God, but *only* the will of God.

MINISTRY AS A WAY OF LIFE

Our time in Dallas has been rich with blessing, despite periods of opposition, discouragement, long hours, and close quarters. Through these things, God has expanded our vision and given us a much broader understanding of the *purposeful but limited* concept of ministry. As I studied the way He "worked," I realized that Jesus saw "ministry" as a way of life. He gave of Himself as He fished with the disciples, taught on a hillside, preached in the temple, walked on the road, and healed the sick. In doing so, He communicated His message of truth in the same way God instructed the Israelites to teach their children. "You shall teach them diligently to your children, and shall talk of them when you sit in your house, and when you walk by the way, and when you lie down, and when you rise." (Deuteronomy 6:7)

When I began to view my work in Dallas as a job, it was easy to find reasons for discouragement and frustration. But, when the Lord opened my eyes and pushed back the mental limitations I had placed on ministry, I could see that His plan for all believers contains so much more than working from nine to five. Our Christianity should so permeate our lives that everything we do "ministers" to those around us. The mindset of ministry should guide us in much the same way that the mindset of motherhood guides a woman with children. Like a mother, a believer should never "clock out" of her responsibility to love those around her. In this way we can accomplish *all* the will of God while staying *only* within the boundaries of our calling.

If we abide in the presence of Christ and then identify and function within our calling, this kind of ministry will flow effortlessly and bless each person we touch. As we abide, we realize what John the Baptist knew, that in order to maximize our potential for God and fulfill His highest calling on our lives, "He (Christ) must increase, but I must decrease." (John 3:30) J. I. Packer has noted, "To trust one's own works alongside the work of Christ dishonors Him, frustrates grace, and cuts one off from life." (God's Words, p.104) The lasting value of our lives is determined by how much of Christ manifests itself through us, not any list of our supposed achievements or accolades.

This book is specifically designed for those who find

themselves on the "works" end of the spectrum, those who are redeemed but driven to exhaustion rather than delight by their zeal for God. However, I hope it will also encourage those who gravitate toward the sidelines to get into the exciting "game" God has set before them. If you are a child of God, you are in the race that He marked out for you before the beginning of time. Your choice is not whether or not to be in the race, but rather, whether you will run gratefully or grudgingly.

I came to God gratefully as a child and my gratitude grew as I learned more of Him and His ways. But, somewhere along the way, I began to resent the way He did things and to presume I knew better than He. I then served Him grudgingly, and began my descent into poor physical, emotional, and spiritual health. The race became one of drudgery rather than one filled with the delights of knowing, loving, and serving God and others. Fortunately, the Lord did not leave me in that state. Recovery – of my spiritual perspective as well as my health – began with the rediscovery of the love that drew me to Christ in the first place. In reawakening to His love, I began to find the blessing within God's boundaries again.

CHAPTER TWO

Accepted before the First Miracle

"Loved with everlasting love,
Led by grace that love to know;
Gracious Spirit from above, Thou has taught me it is so!
O, this full and perfect peace! O, this transport all divine!
In a love which cannot cease, I am His, and He is mine."
George W. Robinson

I began my study of the life of Christ in the fall of 2001, almost exactly a year after my initial diagnosis. Being rather fanatical about organization, I started with the book of Matthew and read straight through each of the gospels. Whenever something stood out, I took time to write it down before continuing. At the conclusion of each book, I inserted the notes into an outline before going on to the next. The study that evolved is not an exhaustive summary of these portions of Scripture by any means, but it excites me to see how God has used it to cover many facets of the Christian life. The first concept that stood out to me defines the most important boundary of all. It must be understood in order to apply the rest and, of all the principles I saw as I studied, it has brought the most profound change and freedom in my life.

THE SEDUCTION OF OVERACHIEVEMENT

As a firstborn who tends to strive for perfection in everything, a strong drive to please my authorities has always motivated my performance. I still remember the heavy heart with which I carried my report card to my parents when I received my first "B," in any subject, in the fourth grade. I always studied to be at the top of my class and worked hard to please parents and teachers alike. My parents never pressured me to achieve certain grades, but rather to do my best. However, the numbers, the averages, and the class placement motivated me. I received the only "C" of my life in a geography class at Messiah and made a special appeal to the professor to reconsider in order not to "destroy" my A/B record as a student!

Somewhere along the way, my performance-based drive to please authorities carried over to my relationship with the Lord. I longed to please Him and thought I needed to attain perfection to do so. While in college, a friend gave me a cross-stitch of Philippians 1:6, "And I am sure of this, that he who began a good work in you will bring it to completion at the day of Jesus Christ." The realization that God, as the initiator of the good work in me, was responsible to complete it comforted me. But, I am sad to say that most of the time I strove to complete the work for Him, not realizing that perfection on this side of the grave is an unattainable – and even unhealthy – goal.

Attempting to set my own limitations, and to set them high, led to constant frustration and disappointment with myself. It also resulted in an inability to fully appreciate praise from others or relax between accomplishments. For two years prior to my diagnosis, I studied, meditated on, and worked toward memorizing Ephesians one and two. During that time, some truths began to crystallize in my thinking, and they burst forth into my conscious reality with clarity when I discovered the first principle of boundaries pertaining to life and ministry that Jesus understood.

GOD'S PLEASURE IN CHRIST

In 1983 during our assignment in Turkey, my parents took Julianne and me on a ten-day tour of the Holy Land. I still remember the day we walked down a dusty, little path and felt the air cool as wind swept gently over the river. We heard splashes and blessings before we spotted the people standing in the water receiving the sacrament of baptism. For many, getting baptized in the Jordan River was a dream come true. As we stood in that historic place, our guide recounted the story of Christ's baptism and the significance of that event.

Matthew, Mark, Luke, and John all describe the baptism of Christ early in their gospels. Matthew 3:17 says, "… and behold, a voice from heaven said, 'This is my beloved Son, with whom I am well pleased'." Mark 1:11 states, "And a voice came from heaven, 'You are my beloved Son; with you I am well pleased'."

And Luke 3:21-22 affirms, "Now when all the people were baptized, and when Jesus also had been baptized and was praying, the heavens were opened, and the Holy Spirit descended on him in bodily form, like a dove; and a voice came from heaven, 'You are my beloved Son; with you I am well pleased'." (John's similar account of the baptism of Christ is found in John 1:29-34.)

How often in Scripture are the exact same words used in correlating passages? Even in the parallel passages of the gospels, variety often exists. But, not in this case. The writers' consistency marks an amazing affirmation of Christ by His Father. The principle that struck me with such force upon reading this is the fact that God's approval of Christ came *before* the first miracle, affirming who He *was* before He *did* anything signaling His miraculous power. If God recognized the significance of Jesus' personhood prior to any kind of amazing performance, could it be that He already approves of me also?

ACCEPTED IN ETERNITY PAST

Not only do the gospels describe God's vivid display of affirmation and love for Christ before His public ministry began, John offers us a description of the Trinity in his first chapter which highlights another important truth: "In the beginning was the Word, and the Word was with God, and the Word was God. He was in the beginning with God. All things were made through him, and without him was not any thing made that was made. In him was life, and the life was the light of men." (John 1:1-4) Jesus was one with the Father and the Holy Spirit in eternity before time began. As such, He has always been and always will be perfectly accepted by God. Later on in John, one of Christ's prayers affirms his understanding of this eternal relationship. He prays in John 17:24 saying, "Father, I desire that they also, whom you have given me, may be with me where I am, to see my glory that you have given me *because you loved me before the foundation of the world."* (emphasis mine)

Because Christ is the "firstborn among many brothers" (Romans 8:29), and those who believe on Him become the children of God and joint-heirs with Him (Romans 8:16-17), we also enjoy God's approval and pleasure based on *who we are* rather than *what we do*. Works must follow legitimate faith, but I should do them out of love and gratefulness, from a place of perfect assurance, rather than grudgingly offer them as my duty or as the wages I pay in hopes of receiving eternal favor.

Recognizing the security of my boundaries here was an

incalculable blessing because it revolutionized my thinking about myself and my relationship with God. Striving for God's acceptance and approval no longer motivates my work, outreach and relationships, because I know I already have them. Hallelujah! The longer I meditate on this amazing truth, the more I realize that He will love me no more on the day of my death than He loved me the day of my birth. I am responsible to use the time between these events wisely, but in the journey of life I am coming to understand who He already says I am, not making a name for myself in heaven.

One afternoon in January of 1991, I stole some time from studies to bundle up and visit one of my favorite places on campus, a swinging bridge suspended over the creek that draws the border between the academic buildings and dorms and the athletic fields. Trees line the sides of the stream and under their branches I found solace many a time when I needed a quiet place to sit and think. My fellowship with the Lord that day inspired me to write the following essay that tells of His unchanging love.

"I Could Never Love You More"

The satin blanket of milky white drapes across the earth, tenderly shielding it from the bitterness of winter.

The bare branches of the trees stretch over the water like fingers grasping toward the sky for a hint of warmth.

The creek flows silently by, cold, icy.

But the sun, the sun shines across the water and sparkles like diamonds spilling over onto the bank and turning to gold.

And God speaks gently to my soul, "My darling, I could never love you more than I do this very moment:

Not in the spring when the grass spreads like a velvety carpet and the flowers blossom while trees brighten to full bloom;

Not in the summer when clouds drift by aimlessly across a never-ending sky of bright blue while tropical breezes caress your face;

And not in autumn when the world bursts with all the rich colors of my imagination and warm breezes turn cool.

I am the Lord and I am the same yesterday, today, and forever. I love you with a love that never ends. I could never love you more."

Many things about God inspire love and adoration in His children. One of the greatest is surely our security in Christ: that He chose us, pursued us until His grace overcame our resistance, and now keeps us safely in His love until we meet Him face to face. Without an accurate understanding of this truth, we are destined to miss the mark God envisioned for us when He prepared our ways before the foundation of the world (see Psalm 139:16). But when this truth permeates our hearts as well as our heads, any grudge toward our "duty" should instantly pale in comparison with our gratitude for God's mercy.

Just as Christ was accepted in eternity and that acceptance affirmed in time, the believer's boundaries are established by God before his physical birth and sealed in the spiritual birth experienced later. In what is called His High Priestly prayer, Jesus beseeched the Father, "I am praying for them. I am not praying for the world but for those whom you have given me, for they are yours. ... I do not ask for these only, but also for those who will believe in me through their word." (John 17:9, 20) Jesus' prayer alludes to the sovereign choices of God and for whom, exactly, Christ prepared to face the cross.

Beginning to grasp the implications of this amazing, and mysterious, theme of Scripture was a key part of the first steps I took toward understanding my position in Christ. Meditating on Ephesians one and two further opened the door for me to begin to comprehend the mystery of God's eternal calling on my life. For two years I memorized a few verses at a time and then meditated on them through the day and as I lay in bed awaiting sleep at night. When I was sick it sometimes took me an hour or two to fall asleep, so I had plenty of time to think on these things. Ephesians 1:4 became a favorite, "even as he chose us in him before the foundation of the world, that we should be holy and blameless before him."

Realizing that I came to Him, through my own choice, but primarily because of His wooing grace and eternal plan for my destiny increased my wonder and trust in God tremendously. I do not understand the mystery of how His will works with mine, but I can certainly agree with Paul as He wrote in Romans 11:33, "Oh, the depth of the riches and wisdom and knowledge of God! How unsearchable are his judgments and how inscrutable his ways!" Though I prayed to receive Christ as a child, these realizations injected a freshness to my faith. It was as if all my life I looked at the world through a curtained window, and someone finally drew back the lace to reveal a more clear view of reality than I had ever seen.

SECURE IN HIS LOVE

The knowledge that the God of the universe chose me for His own in eternity and, at the appointed time, called me to Himself gives me faith that He will also hold me securely in His love throughout my life. In other words, I do not have to fear falling out of His grip. I may let go of Him at times, but He never lets go of me. Jesus said, in John 10:25-29, "...I told you, and you do not believe. The works that I do in my Father's name bear witness about me, but you do not believe because you are not part of my flock. *My sheep hear my voice, and I know them, and they follow me. I give them eternal life, and they will never perish, and no one will snatch them out of my hand. My Father, who has given them to me, is greater than all, and no one is able to snatch them out of the Father's hand."* (emphasis mine)

I firmly believe I never would have chosen Christ on my own. How could someone "dead in sin" (see Romans 6) comprehend a different reality without being acted upon by an outside force? Knowing the deceitfulness of heart and flesh that still remain, despite a redeemed spirit, I recognize that I would lose my salvation if I could. Josiah Conder wrote:

> 'Tis not that I did choose thee, for, Lord that could not be;
> This heart would still refuse thee hadst thou not chosen me.
> Thou from the sin that stained me hast cleansed and set me free;
> Of old thou hast ordained me that I should live to thee.
>
> 'Twas sov'reign mercy called me and taught my op'ning mind;
> The world had else enthralled me, to heav'nly glories blind.
> My heart owns none before thee, for thy rich grace I thirst;
> This knowing, if I love thee, Thou must have loved me first.

Praise God that since He called me, He will also preserve me. Romans 8:38-39 is a familiar reassurance: "For I am sure that neither death nor life, nor angels nor rulers, nor things present nor things to come, nor powers, nor height nor depth, nor anything else in all creation, will be able to separate us from the love of God in Christ Jesus our Lord."

Assurance is also found in the familiar words of Psalm 23. Several years ago I read Phillip Keller's book, <u>A Shepherd Looks at Psalm 23</u>. In it, he explains applications gleaned from his years tending sheep in South Africa. His insights helped me understand the significance of this passage in new ways.

Perhaps most pertinent to this discussion is the fact that the shepherd chooses his sheep and provides for them. He alone sets the boundaries for his flock. *"The LORD is my Shepherd; I shall not want."* (verse 1) Sheep do not choose their own master or their own fields. In like manner, the Shepherd of the universe gathers His sheep to Himself, leads them to their proper pasture and takes care of their needs. Sheep are fairly helpless and have a reputation for stupidity – not a very flattering comparison for the Christian – but one that should help us better see ourselves as God does.

Throughout the psalm we see illustrations of the shepherd caring for the sheep. He makes sure they have fresh food and clean water, a place to walk and a place to rest. He protects them from danger and disciplines as needed for their own safety and benefit. I saw these principles vividly when the Lord allowed illness into my life that forced me to slow down and rest. I knew how to *do* but scarcely remembered how to *be*. I had to allow Him to refresh my body and restore my soul, drawing my mind, will, and emotions so close to His own that I responded to His heartbeat, the tap – rather than the slap – of His staff.

Verse three says, " ... He leads me in the paths of righteousness *for His name's sake.*" (emphasis mine) Just as the shepherd protects His reputation by caring for the sheep in his care, God shelters His own for the sake of His name. He leads me in the right way for my benefit, yes, but also for

His glory. Since we know He will not neglect the praise and glory of His own name, we can rest assured of His faithful care for us. Just like the sheep receive the best care in the pasture of their shepherd, so the believer experiences his richest blessing within the boundaries established by God.

David closes the psalm with the beautiful promise of eternal security in the home of the Great Shepherd: "Surely goodness and mercy shall follow me all the days of my life: and I shall dwell in the house of the LORD forever" (verse 6). Just as a shepherd desires to return all his sheep safely to the fold, the Lord God intends to bring each of His own to their eternal place in heaven.

Passage after passage of Scripture assures me that the burden of responsibility is His. Isaiah 49:15-16 says, "Can a woman forget her nursing child, that she should have no compassion on the son of her womb? Even these may forget, *yet I will not forget you.* Behold, I have engraved you on the palms of my hands; your walls are continually before me." (emphasis mine) Even if it were possible for a mother to neglect her nursing infant, the Almighty God will not forget or neglect His children. This reference also alludes to Christ's sacrifice on the cross, where soldiers symbolically "engraved" His people into His hands for all eternity.

Psalm 138: 7-8 is a personal favorite: "Though I walk in the midst of trouble, you preserve my life; you stretch out your hand against the wrath of my enemies, and your right hand delivers me. The Lord will fulfill his purpose for me; your steadfast love, O Lord, endures forever. Do not forsake the work of your hands." My responsibility is to rest within the boundaries of God's love and allow Him to save, perfect and preserve me. My soul does the resting and my actions should reflect a grateful response to the grace I have received.

CHOSEN WITH A PURPOSE

The fact that God chose us for a reason and imbued us

with a mission is as certain as our eternal security within the boundaries of His love. Works come after the acceptance by God; Ephesians 2:8-9 make this very clear. "For by grace you have been saved through faith. And this is not your own doing; it is the gift of God, not a result of works, so that no one may boast." If salvation were possible to earn, it could never be called a gift. Ephesians 2:10 follows, "For we are his workmanship, created in Christ Jesus for good works, which God prepared beforehand, that we should walk in them."

I memorized this passage during my mission trip to England and Scotland, but only through this study have I come to rest completely in the assurance that I can never earn salvation. To attempt to do so insults the One who offers it freely. It is God's gift to me and I honor Him by simply accepting it, not by constantly working to prove that I, in some way, merit His choice.

"You did not choose me, but I chose you and appointed you that you should go and bear fruit and that your fruit should abide, so that whatever you ask the Father in my name, He may give it to you." (John 15:16) God does have works in store for me, but I do not have to find them for myself. My challenge is to know Him so intimately that the ordained path is obvious. Proverbs 3:5-6 admonishes me to "Trust in the Lord with all your heart, and do not lean on your own understanding. In all your ways acknowledge Him, and He will make straight your paths." As I rest in the soil of His will and drink from the fountain of His wisdom, the fruit will grow naturally, according to His design.

God reassured me of His choice during my African adventure. During that summer on the coast of Liberia, our leaders occasionally let us swim at the end of a long day of mixing mortar and laying bricks for the house we were building. One afternoon after jumping over chest-high waves long enough to grow weary, a large surge caught me as I waded toward the shore. After throwing me forward and pushing me down, the water tumbled me over, like clothes in a dryer, until I no longer knew sky from sand. My lungs felt like they would burst and scenes from my life flashed across my eyelids. With an internal cry for direction, I lunged forward and fortunately burst through water to air.

I struggled for my footing and staggered up the shore before collapsing out of reach of the now-menacing waves. I knew I had come close to death and sensed that God spared me for a purpose. He had my undivided attention, and I asked Him for a Scripture verse to reassure me of His presence and protection. During my quiet time later in the week, I came across Isaiah 54, a passage describing the future city of Jerusalem. Verse 11 begins, "O afflicted one, storm-tossed and not comforted ..." Those verses leapt out at me because I had been tossed and, even a few days later, still needed comforting. The passage goes on to describe how God intends to establish the city and promises to prosper and protect its inhabitants. On that day, He used it to assure me of His hand of protection upon my life and His desire to bless me and use me in the future. In that moment, I knew the safest place to be was the center of His will. I could believe the truth of Jim Elliot's statement, "Each man is immortal until his life's work is done."

Since that summer, anytime I have been fearful of the future or unsure of my path, I have returned to this passage and found comfort. God's promises never change. They do not waver like waves on the water, but are sure and sound like rocks beneath the sand on the shore. Whether the challenges are threats to my physical life or just to my emotional well-being, I am at peace as long as I remember His promises.

THE SOURCE OF ULTIMATE APPROVAL AND ETERNAL REWARD

In addition to reveling in God's acceptance and plan for my life, I need to look to Him, rather than others, for both approval and reward. Proverbs 29:25 says, "The fear of man lays a snare, but whoever trusts in the Lord is safe." Jesus set a consistent example by always looking to God, not man, for approval. Christ believed the truth of this proverb explicitly and his actions underscored his understanding.

Had He just desired to please others, Christ likely would have conducted His business differently. Perhaps He would have healed more of the sick and financially prospered the people living under the harsh rule of the Roman Empire. Speaking out against the tyranny of the emperor would surely have been more popular with the religious elite than focusing His displeasure on them. However, Christ was not bound by the people's expectations or deterred from His purpose when they rejected Him. He knew His ultimate approval rested in God's hands, not theirs. When they turned against Him, He moved on to the next place, the next group, the next step down the path His Father ordained for Him before the beginning of time. He refused to indulge in bitterness when they turned away, forgiving even his executioners and the repentant thief on the cross.

Jesus also knew His real reward and recognition would be from God in heaven, not on earth. In Luke 14 He tells the parable of the wedding feast where guests are seated in different rooms according to their rank of honor in the eyes of the host. He challenges His followers to seek the places of lesser honor and to humble themselves, to wait for others to promote them to a higher position rather than prematurely claiming it. Later in the same chapter, He exhorts them to invite "the poor, the crippled, the lame and the blind" to their parties rather than welcoming only the rich and popular. He reminds them that the responsibility of believers is to court the undesirable rather than seeking the approval of the elite. He closes the lesson on humility by saying, "…and you will be blessed, because they cannot repay you. You will be repaid at the resurrection of the just." We should pursue the

Father's approval and His recognition, not the paltry rewards humans can bestow.

As Jesus instructed the disciples for their earthly benefit, He must have known these principles would most appropriately relate to Him. What recognition could He expect on earth that could begin to compare with the honor awaiting His return to heaven? He humbled Himself beyond what we can begin to imagine. Philippians 2:5-9 describe His humility as He sets the example for us all. "Have this mind among yourselves, which is yours in Christ Jesus, who, though he was in the form of God, did not count equality with God a thing to be grasped, but made himself nothing, taking the form of a servant, being born in the likeness of men. And being found in human form, he humbled himself by becoming obedient to the point of death, even death on a cross. Therefore God has highly exalted him and bestowed on him the name that is above every name ...".

When we follow the example of Christ, we can be assured of eternal reward as well. Colossians 3:1 tells us that we are already in a position to experience the blessing of God because we are "risen with Christ" and thus seated with Him "on the right hand of God." Ephesians 1:3 says, "Blessed be the God and Father of our Lord Jesus Christ, who has blessed us in Christ with every spiritual blessing in the heavenly places." Although we do not physically relate to our position this side of the grave, we can learn to walk in the overwhelming spiritual blessings God gives us through Christ.

John Piper writes in his classic work <u>Desiring God</u>, "Deep within us we all know that it is our duty to glorify our Maker by thanking Him for all we have, trusting Him for all we need, and obeying all His revealed will." (p.56) Christ set the perfect example for us when He glorified the Father through obedience to every aspect of His will. He rested within the boundaries of His eternal acceptance and reflected His God-given purpose at every turn. In the same way, I should delight in my security in Christ and live each day in gratefulness that God called me to Himself, saved me for His glory, equipped me for a unique purpose, and even now prepares an eternal reward for me to enjoy with Him in heaven. What blessedness lies within the boundaries of His sovereign will!

CHAPTER THREE

How to Identify
Your Life Calling

*"For we are his workmanship, created in Christ Jesus
for good works, which God prepared beforehand,
that we should walk in them."*
Ephesians 2:10

In order to walk joyfully within the boundaries God designed for His children, it helps to know and understand the purposes for which He created us. In the context of this book, I will refer to this purpose as "life calling." Understanding God's call on my life has helped me to define the boundaries within which I experience the most joy and effectiveness as a person. In this chapter, I describe the process by which I came to understand these boundaries and the blessing of operating within them. I hope these insights help you to discern God's purposes for placing *you* on earth at this particular time in human history, with your unique set of relationships and circumstances. Now that we have been reminded that neither you nor I am here to run the universe, let's consider what God has put us here to do. As in Chapter Two, we begin with a look at the life of Christ.

Thoroughly understanding His life calling enabled Christ to maximize His time on Earth. When Nicodemus visits Him by night to question His teaching, miracles, and ultimately His origin, Christ informs him, "For God so loved the world, that he gave his only Son, that whoever believes in him should not perish but have eternal life. For God did not send his Son into the world to condemn the world, but in order that the world might be saved through him." (John 3:16-17) Christ's ability to articulate this indicates that He recognized and embraced his role as Savior of mankind.

When asked to read the Scriptures during a Sabbath meeting in the synagogue in his hometown of Nazareth, Jesus found the passage in Isaiah describing Himself, "The Spirit of the Lord is upon me, because he has anointed me to proclaim good news to the poor. He has sent me to proclaim liberty to the captives and recovering of sight to the blind, to set at liberty those who are oppressed, to proclaim the year of the Lord's favor." (Luke 4:18 – 19) This not only demonstrated knowledge of the Scriptures, but more importantly, an understanding of how Scripture specifically described and applied to Him. Because He understood His mission (His boundaries), Christ changed the world and altered eternity like no one who has lived before or since. Given this fact, His comment in John 14:12 should arrest our attention, "Truly, truly, I say to you, whoever believes in me will also do the works that I do; and greater works than these will he do, because I am going to the Father."

What an amazing statement! God has greater works for us – His children – to do than even Christ performed. If I believe the verity of this statement, it follows that I should seek to know this individual charge so that I can obey God by doing it. Determining my life calling over the course of several years has significantly impacted the way I live each day by giving me a defining sense of purpose and security in knowing that God designed me to fulfill a specific task to help extend His eternal kingdom. Though, in this chapter, we will try to lay a foundation for what we *do* and how we live, let us not forget that our ultimate blessing lies in glorifying God by *being* the person He knew and loved before the foundation of the world.

GOD'S GOAL FOR HIS CHILDREN

Before we can begin to understand the spiritual significance of our lives, we must first understand God's ultimate goal for His children. Jesus' words to Nicodemus in John 3:16 proclaim God's motivation and desire, "For God so loved the world, that he gave his only Son, that whoever believes in him should not perish but have eternal life." In one passage of many describing God's pursuit of His people, Peter writes, "The Lord is not slow to fulfill his promise as some count slowness, but is patient toward you, not wishing that any should perish, but that all should reach repentance." (II Peter 3:9) So, God's ultimate *goal* in our lives is that we know Him through the saving grace of Christ and put our faith and trust in Him for life and for all eternity.

After the free gift of God's grace through Christ transforms our souls, God desires for us to live a life consecrated to Him. To enable this, God blesses His children with ALL spiritual blessings through Christ (Ephesians 1:3). In Ephesians 1:1, Paul refers to believers as "saints:" those who are holy, set apart, sanctified, consecrated; and as "faithful:" certain, worthy to be believed; true, just, and trustworthy. He describes His own as chosen before time began, adopted as God's children with all the rights and privileges of a son or daughter of the King. His grace makes us acceptable in every way. We do not have to act in a certain manner to earn His love, but rather His love should motivate a change in our behavior. This is the legacy of those who accept God's free gift of pardon through the substitutionary atonement of Christ.

From these saints, God desires total dedication. Paul writes in Romans 12:1-2, "I appeal to you therefore, brothers, by the mercies of God, to present your bodies as a living sacrifice, holy and acceptable to God, which is your spiritual worship. Do not be conformed to this world, but be transformed by the renewal of your mind, that by testing you may discern what is the will of God, what is good and acceptable and perfect." He begs the Roman Christians to alter their lifestyles in a very reasonable response to Christ's sacrifice for them. This passage highlights the mark of true believers, not those who are perfect, but those who display their inner redemption with outward change. True believers desire to spend time with God. They strive to live holy lives, fully consecrated to Him. They accept His design for their lives spiritually, emotionally and physically. Finally, they busy themselves studying to learn what pleases God.

THE BELIEVER'S PURPOSE FOR LIVING

If the aforementioned qualities characterize our lives, then we can know for sure that we belong to God. At that point, it is pertinent to ask the question, what is our *life purpose* as believers? The Westminster Confession answers the question in the following way: to glorify God and enjoy Him forever. John Piper restates this: the believer's purpose is to glorify God *by* enjoying Him forever.

Both statements are grounded in Scriptures such as Psalm 86:11-13 which says, "Teach me your way, O Lord, that I may walk in your truth; unite my heart to fear your name. I give thanks to you, O Lord my God, with my whole heart, and I will glorify your name forever. For great is your steadfast love toward me; you have delivered my soul from the depths of Sheol." Jesus instructs in Matthew 5:16, "In the same way, let your light shine before others, so that they may see your good works and give glory to your Father who is in heaven." Paul tells the Corinthians, "... for you were bought with a price. So glorify God in your body." (I Corinthians 6:20).

THE GOAL OF EVERY BELIEVER

So, all Christians have the same *life purpose*: to glorify God. The *life goal* of every believer is also the same: to grow in a relationship with the living God through His Son and our Savior, Jesus Christ. Paul summarizes our goal in Philippians 3:10, "that I may know him and the power of his resurrection, and may share his sufferings, becoming like him in his death."

This is a process, begun in time and completed in eternity. Our love for Christ should motivate us to follow Him daily, heeding the admonition of Paul: "Not that I have already obtained this or am already perfect, but I press on to make it my own, because Christ Jesus has made me his own. Brothers, I do not consider that I have made it my own. But one thing I do: forgetting what lies behind and straining forward to what lies ahead, I press on toward the goal for the prize of the upward call of God in Christ Jesus." (Philippians 3:12 – 14) As we glorify God and pursue a relationship with Him, we are changed into the likeness of Christ. This, in turn, points others to God.

A VARIETY OF CALLINGS

So, the life purpose and goal of every Christian are the same. As we are transformed more and more into the image of Christ, we are equipped for our life calling. This *life calling* is to share the gospel and make disciples. Before returning to heaven, Jesus clearly instructed His followers to do this work. Matthew 28:19-20 records His final admonition, "Go therefore and make disciples of all nations, baptizing them in the name of the Father and of the Son and of the

Holy Spirit, teaching them to observe all that I have commanded you. And behold, I am with you always, to the end of the age." Mark 16:15 echoes the instruction in Matthew, "Go into all the world and proclaim the gospel to the whole creation." And Luke repeats the command in Acts 1:8, "But you will receive power when the Holy Spirit has come upon you, and you will be my witnesses in Jerusalem and in all Judea and Samaria, and to the end of the earth."

The salvation and discipleship of those who do not know Christ should concern every believer. A desire for others to believe on Christ is indeed evidence of our own saving faith. Psalm 71:15-16 says, "My mouth will tell of your righteous acts, of your deeds of salvation all the day, for their number is past my knowledge. With the mighty deeds of the Lord God I will come; I will remind them of your righteousness, yours alone." However, the Holy Spirit will lead each Christian to witness to a particular group of people. This is the practical outworking of the concept of the Church as a body. Just as each part of the body is designed for a different purpose and fashioned to fulfill a different function, so God calls believers to impact the world in different ways. "But as it is, God arranged the members in the body, each one of them, as he chose." (I Corinthians 12:18)

This is where our boundaries change from the general commands for every believer to the specific focus of individual lives. For instance, Paul spent the bulk of his ministry evangelizing the Gentiles. Peter focused his energies on the Jews. In more recent history we have examples such as Hudson Taylor who followed God's call to the Chinese, Amy Carmichael who gave her life for the orphans of India, and David Livingston who pioneered mission work in Africa. God called Chuck Colson, the founder of Prison Fellowship Ministries, to bring the gospel to men and women in jail. Some are called to work with children, some with youth, others with the elderly or widows or pregnant

teens. The list is as long as the imagination because God lit-
erally loves all kinds of people and commands all believers
to commit to the cause of proclaiming this good news.

DEVELOPING YOUR "TENT-MAKING" SKILLS

So, the believer's *purpose* is to glorify God, her *goal*: to
grow in the image of Christ, and her *calling*: to reach out to
whichever group God lays upon her heart. Notice that this
part of the Christian "race" is not optional. We glorify God,
grow in our knowledge of Christ, and participate in the
Great Commission, or we live in disobedience.

Assuming we are seeking to live lives of obedience,
how do we make this practical on a day-to-day basis? We
start by identifying our *life work*. A believer's *life work* is
whatever he does that enables him to fulfill God's call on
his life. The work may seem strictly "spiritual" such as pas-
toring a church, teaching in a seminary, or writing books to
nurture and teach believers. Or, the work may seem "secu-
lar," like Paul making tents in order to help offset the cost
of his missionary journeys. But in truth, all work is spiritual
if done to the glory of God and with the goal of furthering
His kingdom.

HOW TO DETERMINE YOUR LIFE CALLING

Understanding the purpose and goal of the Christian life
is not difficult because they are reinforced and clarified from
Genesis to Revelation. God has set the boundaries clearly.
Determining one's life work can be a challenge, but it can
also be as simple as asking, "What do I enjoy doing?" Or,
"In what areas do my talents, gifts, and abilities lie?" The
real difficulty I have found is zeroing in on a particular
group of people and articulating a call with confidence. Let
me outline some steps that have helped me determine the
boundaries of my life calling.

Step One - Pray

The first and most important step is to pray. God never hides His will from a seeking heart. Matthew 7:7-8 says, "Ask, and it will be given to you; seek, and you will find; knock, and it will be opened to you. For everyone who asks receives, and the one who seeks finds, and to the one who knocks it will be opened." It may take time to recognize God's answer, but He promises to hear and respond to our prayers. No one wants us to go about the business of fulfilling His calling on our lives more than He does. Keep in mind that God will not call you to do anything that contradicts the commands and principles already outlined in Scripture.

Step Two – Trust God to Direct You

A second step is to acknowledge God in all things. Proverbs 3:5-6 says, "Trust in the Lord with all your heart, and do not lean on your own understanding. In all your ways acknowledge him, and he will make straight your paths." Determining direction for life requires a great deal of trust, and trust is a weighty issue. God longs to reveal His will to us, but more than that, He wants us to learn to trust Him and His wisdom above our own.

Recently, I read the story in II Kings 1 of the wicked Israelite king, Ahaziah. This son of Ahab and Jezebel fell ill and sent his servants on an urgent errand: to inquire of a false god regarding his health. On the way, they met the prophet Elijah who sent them back to the king with these words, "Is it because there is no God in Israel that you are going to inquire of Baal-zebub, the god of Ekron?" At first blush, I thought this passage irrelevant to me, but upon prayer and reflection, I saw a deep significance. Ahaziah exemplifies the independent human spirit in all of us that tends to bypass the availability of Almighty God and instead looks for guidance from so called idols.

In this area of life calling, I spent years going my own

way, like a traveler trying to find a forgotten path in the dark. I forgot that the One who created light longs to brighten my path and make His way for my life clear. When I stumbled along the way, too often I had the tendency of Ahaziah to look to friends, culture, and my own wisdom for answers rather than asking God to show me the way. As I begin to look to Him for guidance in all things, He is leading me in the path He has already prepared. On this path, the calling is clear and I can march forward with confidence.

Step Three – Begin to Obey

God has given many commands in Scripture, and a third step toward defining a life calling is to begin doing the things He commands everyone. This is how to "walk in the way" while awaiting specific direction. The following is a brief list of some major directives and questions to consider:

- Revelation 2:5 – *Repent and do works motivated by your first love.* Do I walk in an attitude of repentance, focusing on loving Christ and doing works motivated, first and foremost, by my love for Him?
- James 5:16 – *Confess and pray.* Have I humbled myself recently, confessing my struggles to other believers and praying with and for them? Edward Welch has written, "If you really want to lay a foundation for honesty, you must be a person who is quick to acknowledge your own sin, and who will not overreact to sin in those close to you." (Addictions, p.95)
- Habakkuk 2:4 – *Live by faith.* Am I living by the faith God gives me, trusting Him and living by the truths of His Word?
- I Thessalonians 5:16 – *Rejoice in all things.* Do I choose joy in my circumstances or waste energy in complaining and discontentment?
- Ephesians 6:1 – *Honor your parents.* Do I spend time

with my parents and do the things they ask me to do?

- I Peter 3:1 – *If married, honor your husband.* Do I reverence my husband and honor him as the head of our home?
- Matthew 9:37-38 – *Pray for unbelievers.* How concerned am I with the billions who have never heard the name of Christ?
- Galatians 6:10 – *Do good to all, especially other Christians.* Do I look for practical ways to strengthen the faith of other believers and to help meet their needs?

This is just a quick, yet hopefully thought-provoking, list of general commands. At times in the past I have made lists of things God commands everyone as I read through Scripture during my devotional times. I would heartily suggest that you undertake such a study as well. I believe the length of the list will likely amaze you and give you plenty of ideas for how to begin walking in the direction of discovering and understanding your unique calling.

Oswald Chambers made the statement, "All God's revelations are sealed until they are opened to us by obedience … God will never reveal more truth about Himself until you have obeyed what you know already." (My Utmost for His Highest, October 10) If you are unsure about your calling, could it be that the Lord is waiting to see how serious you are about following Him before providing more specifics? Perhaps you (and I) need to apply what we know and trust God to reveal the rest in His time. Scripture assures us that He will. I firmly believe that He never hides His will from a seeking heart.

Before going further, let me share a word of caution. Lists can be dangerous … as you study Scripture and look for God's direction, do not become overwhelmed and try to do everything at once. There is more to believe and obey in God's Word than we can possibly learn and apply this side of the grave. I would encourage you to choose one or two things to begin prayerfully focusing on and allow the Holy Spirit to prompt you to add to that at an appropriate time.

Boundaries lead to freedom, not to checklists of dos and don'ts. As we walk in obedience, our foremost goal must be to increase in the knowledge of Christ. Otherwise, our desire to obey may actually lead us into bondage. "When principles or steps wander from Christ Himself, they become self-serving guidelines. They may make our marriages, families, friendships and work go better, but the goal is our own betterment more than the glory of God." (Welch, Addictions, p.155) When we begin to live by checklists rather than relishing our relationship with Christ, we lean toward the Law rather than living by grace.

Step Four – Ask God to Confirm His Calling Through His Word

Sooner or later, you will begin to have an idea of your calling. At that point, it is wise to ask God to give specific verses of Scripture to confirm it. As I have pondered my life calling over the years, I have asked the Lord to highlight verses that apply specifically to His purposes for my life during the course of my regular reading and studying of the Scriptures. God's direction is found as the Holy Spirit illuminates His written word, so that is the best place to look for it.

Step Five – Seek Wise Counsel

Another important step toward solidifying the direction of your calling involves asking others for confirmation. God gives special wisdom to parents for their children and sometimes teachers for their students, and pastors for their parishioners. Those who know you best can serve as a sounding board as you seek your way in this important area.

I began praying about my life calling while in college. At that time I thought my life work would be teaching children, so I studied for a degree in elementary education. The teachers I consulted in high school concurred with this direction. I also believed God was preparing me to be a wife and mother, which I think is His plan for most women. My parents agreed with my overall focus, and supported my pursuit of this degree as a tool to enable my life work. However, during a seminar, I was also challenged by a Christian leader's counsel to pray about a vision for life that I could fulfill whether single or married. This motivated me to really pursue this aspect of my calling in order to discover and understand it.

During my junior year, a man spoke in one of our bi-weekly chapel services and shared about the call God had given him for discipleship. For the first time, I realized that Matthew 28:19-20 really emphasizes training and teaching rather than evangelism. This message rang true in my heart, and I believed God was calling me to disciple young women. The Scripture was clear regarding discipleship and I believed the focus on other young women was a natural fit. I knew I could begin right away; my position as a resident assistant gave me a perfect opportunity to rub shoulders with those less mature in the Lord. But, for added confirmation, I asked the Lord to send someone for me to encourage in the faith. In the meantime, I began reading a book about discipleship and meditating on Matthew 28.

Not many days later, God answered my prayer. As I sat on the floor studying in my dorm room, I heard a soft knock at the door. I opened it and a young woman, a freshman on my floor, stood outside. She smiled as she introduced herself by saying, "Hi! My name is Jen. Would you be willing to disciple me?" "Hallelujah!" My heart cried as I gladly invited her in and agreed to mentor her. Over the next months, Jen and I met on a weekly basis and shared what God was teaching us in our personal quiet times. We memorized Scripture and prayed together. Our lives influenced one another "as iron sharpening iron," and God began to flesh out a philosophy of discipleship that guides me to this day. It has given me great joy to see Jen catch a vision for discipleship and go on to influence the lives of many others since that time as well.

When I moved to Dallas, the Lord provided countless opportunities to intentionally and unintentionally invest in the lives of others. One of the things I enjoy most is teaching classes for Advanced EXCEL on the topics of discipleship and using time wisely. My goal is to open the eyes of my students to the importance of obeying God's command to disciple whatever groups of people He lays upon their hearts in the same way the chapel speaker opened mine all those years ago. As I watch how this truth influences their lives by expanding their vision, I have come to firmly believe that understanding the boundaries of one's life calling is a necessary part of living a productive life for God's kingdom.

AN ORGANIZED APPROACH

Skip Ryan, the senior pastor at my home church, preached a sermon on this topic in December 2001. He challenged us to take an inventory of the special verses God has given us over the years, the talents and abilities we have developed, and the things we enjoy. Then, he urged us to use this list as a benchmark for measuring the ways in which we spend our time and earn our money. Though I previously had given quite a bit of thought to my life calling and work, this approach encouraged me to reevaluate my priorities. In the following pages, I want to share the process I walked through in hopes that it motivates you and gives you a guide for processing these things for yourself.

Take Inventory of Special Verses

First, I wrote out all of the verses of Scripture that have stood out to me that relate to my life calling. After each one, I listed the specific area, skill, talent, or gifting to which it pertains. Incidentally, for several years I have asked the Lord to give me a special verse or passage at the beginning of January that provides guidance for the coming year. Each time I have prayed this, the Holy Spirit has been faithful to impress on me one or more verses as I read through the Bible during my regular quiet times. So, my list has grown proportionally, just in the last few years, to include the following passages.

Philippians 1:6, "And I am sure of this, that he who began a good work in you will bring it to completion at the day of Jesus Christ." This verse gives me a general assurance of God's presence in my life and commitment to continue refining me after the image of His Son.

Matthew 28:19-20, "Go therefore and make disciples of all nations, baptizing them in the name of the Father and of the Son and of the Holy Spirit, teaching them to observe all that I have commanded you. And behold, I am with you always, to the end of the age." As I mentioned before, this passage confirmed my call to teaching and discipleship while attending college.

I referenced Isaiah 54:10-17 in Chapter Two. The Lord used this passage to comfort me after I nearly drowned in Africa. "For the mountains may depart and the hills be removed, but my steadfast love shall not depart from you, and my covenant of peace shall not be removed,' says the Lord, who has compassion on you. 'O afflicted one, storm-tossed and not comforted, behold, I will set your stones in antimony, and lay your foundations with sapphires. I will make your pinnacles of agate, your gates of carbuncles, and all your walls of precious stones. All your children shall be taught by the Lord, and great shall be the peace of your children. In righteousness you shall be established; you shall be far from oppression, for you shall not fear; and from terror, for it shall not come near you. If anyone stirs up strife, it is not from me; whoever stirs up strife with you shall fall because of you. Behold, I have created the smith who blows the fire of coals and produces a weapon for its purpose. I have also created the ravager to destroy; no weapon that is fashioned against you shall succeed, and you shall confute every tongue that rises against you in judgment. This is the heritage of the servants of the Lord and their vindication from me, declares the Lord."

This passage affirms my love for children and desire for marriage. It reminds me of God's commitment to protect my life until His work through me on this earth is complete. I also have a love for Jewish people, and since the Lord initially directed this passage toward the Hebrews, it increases my sense of identification with them. Last year, I took a course in interior design, and one of the instructors used this passage to illustrate how God affirmed her calling to that field. The structure God describes in this passage sounds breathtaking in its beauty and design. Her comments made me realize this passage relates to that love of mine as well.

Proverbs 24:3-4 says, "By wisdom a house is built, and by understanding it is established; by knowledge the rooms are filled with all precious and pleasant riches." God first impressed me with these verses during a summer music ministry trip in 1991. They mention the areas of home and family, which have always been important to me, as well as alluding to the art of decorating.

Psalm 138 reflects my love for music and challenges me to always use my ability to sing for the Lord. It also speaks about "the kings of the earth" which corresponds with my interest in serving government leaders. Verse 8 correlates with Philippians 1:6, and confirms the applicability of both passages for me. "I give you thanks, O Lord, with my whole heart; before the gods I sing your praise; I bow down toward your holy temple and give thanks to your name for your steadfast love and your faithfulness, for you have exalted above all things your name and your word. On the day I called, you answered me; my strength of soul you increased. All the kings of the earth shall give you thanks, O Lord, for they have heard the words of your mouth, and they shall sing of the ways of the Lord, for great is the glory of the Lord. For though the Lord is high, he regards the lowly, but the haughty he knows from afar. Though I walk in the midst of trouble, you preserve my life; you stretch out your hand against the wrath of my enemies, and your right hand delivers me. The Lord will fulfill his purpose for me; your steadfast love, O Lord, endures forever. Do not forsake the work of your hands."

Psalm 104:33-34 says, "I will sing to the Lord as long as I live; I will sing praise to my God while I have being. May my meditation be pleasing to him, for I rejoice in the Lord." These verses also reflect my love for music, particularly singing.

I was fairly certain my calling was to disciple young ladies, but a study of Titus 2:3-5 in 1994 confirmed this for me. Paul writes, "Older women likewise are to be reverent in behavior, not slanderers or slaves to much wine. They are to teach what is good, and so train the young women to love their husbands and children, to be self-controlled, pure, working at home, kind, and submissive to their own husbands, that the word of God may not be reviled." Although I cannot share from personal experience of marriage at this time, I believe that I can implement the mindset of ministry with those younger than me in either age or spiritual maturity.

Look for Themes

After listing these passages and writing out brief explanations for them, I went back over them looking for themes. The following ones emerged:

1. Salvation – God had called me to Him and confirmed my place in His covenant family.
2. Discipleship/teaching – This is a command for every

believer with a specific call for me to work with younger women.

3. Music – I have loved music for as long as I can remember. These passages confirm that God gifted and called me specifically in the areas of singing and worshipping Him using music.

4. Decorating – This is a practical skill that enables me to make my home a welcoming place to practice hospitality for those that God sends across my path.

5. Home/Marriage/Family – This is a calling that God will fulfill by sending the right man at the right time.

6. Public life – Government has interested me since I first joined the College Republicans as a freshman at Messiah. This corresponds with God's command to all believers in I Timothy 2:1-2, "First of all, then, I urge that supplications, prayers, intercessions, and thanksgivings be made for all people, for kings and all who are in high positions, that we may lead a peaceful and quiet life, godly and dignified in every way."

7. Love for Jewish people – I have a great appreciation for this group of people, the nation through which God brought forth Christ.

Evaluate Activities

Now that I have a list of themes for my calling, based on specific passages of Scripture, I use that to evaluate my activities. This is the third step toward ensuring that the ways I earn money and spend my time accurately reflect God's priorities for my life. If I take inventory of my life and see that I am not using my time in ways that best fit God's call, then I need to consider making changes. This list also serves as a benchmark for evaluating new activities and opportunities. Do they fit with the calling? If not, then I may need to pass. If yes, then I need to consider if I have time to add this new thing to my schedule and still fulfill the commitments already in place.

One thing that will become evident if you do this exercise is that God will confirm many of the things that you enjoy. This is important. For many years, I felt that if I enjoyed something, I somehow earned brownie points with the Lord by laying it aside when my schedule was full. This is a lie designed by Satan to steal our joy.

Psalm 37 is one of my favorite psalms. Verse 4 instructs, "Delight yourself in the Lord, and he will give you the desires of your heart." You can interpret this verse in a couple of ways. In one way, when we delight in God He fulfills the desires of our hearts. In other words, He gives us the things we long for. This is often true, but I find another view to be even more helpful in understanding this verse. As I delight myself in God, He actually *places* desires in my heart, and *then* fulfills them. The greatest desire He gives is a desire for Himself. God told Abraham in Genesis 15:1, "I am thy shield, and thy exceeding great reward." (KJV) Psalm 84:2 says, " … my heart and flesh sing for joy to the living God."

Not pursuing the godly desires that, directly or indirectly, bring us joy is foolish, yet I believe many Christians miss this. I certainly did, and that contributed greatly to my physical illness and emotional depression. While discussing the issue of worship, John Piper writes in <u>Desiring God</u>, "We have implied in a thousand ways that the virtue of an act diminishes to the degree you enjoy doing it, and that doing something because it yields happiness is bad. The notion hangs like a gas in the Christian atmosphere." (pg.89) For many years I viewed my talents, gifts and abilities in this way. If too many activities or responsibilities crowded my schedule, I felt that setting aside the things I loved most was the virtuous and noble thing to do. Only in recent months have I come to see how Satan used this wrong mindset to hinder ministry and stifle joy.

One of my greatest delights is singing. Throughout high

school and college I sang in choirs, small groups, and ensembles. Many times I sang solos as part of group presentations and chapel services at school. One particular highlight was singing the role of Fiona when Messiah produced the musical <u>Brigadoon</u> my junior year. Whether singing before small groups or thousands, worshiping God through music delighted my soul and directed my spirit toward my Maker.

I never questioned the appropriateness of singing solos, or my joy in them. However, several years ago I overheard a conversation that altered my willingness to sing. Let me preface this by saying that the speakers did not address their remarks to me personally, and I sincerely hope they did not intend their words to spark the changes I made. At any rate, as they talked about music they commented that they did not favor having soloists sing because they believed that soloists drew too much attention to themselves and distracted listeners from God.

I had never considered my singing a distraction to anyone and had always prayed that my voice and message would point people to Christ. I loved singing for the Lord and others, but this conversation caused me to question my motives. I thought, "Maybe I love this so much because I get glory from it and the pleasure I feel is self-serving rather than worshipful." From that time on, I drew back from singing in front of people. I turned down opportunities to sing when asked and instead channeled my love for music into directing choirs and occasionally singing in small groups.

As I second-guessed my motives, a part of me shriveled up inside, almost without my realizing it, until a few years ago when I began singing in the choir at my church. Weekly rehearsals and services on Sunday quickly became the highlights of my week. I felt more alive while singing and jokingly referred to it as "therapy" for my illness. Strangers began approaching me after church and commenting on the joy they saw on my countenance when I sang and how much that impressed them. At first that made me nervous; perhaps I distracted them? Then, I realized that God was using my love for singing to point others to Him in worship, just as I always prayed He would do.

One day as I thought about my renewed joy in music, I remembered a conversation from the movie, "Chariots of Fire." In this particular scene Eric Liddell talks with his sister and she berates him for spending so much time training to run in the Olympics when he could be preaching instead. He replies to her queries with a statement something like this: "God made me fast. And when I run, I feel His pleasure." I realized that God had given me the talent of singing. And when I sing, I feel pleasure, both His and my own. Therefore, singing is a good and valid part of my calling and the fact that I enjoy it only heightens my effectiveness.

As I close this chapter, I hope you will take some time to reflect on Scriptures that have become meaningful to you over the years. Evaluate them, meditate on them again, and ask God to give you fresh insights regarding their application to your life. Make lists of the areas in which you have an interest and ability. Then use these to evaluate the ways in which you spend your time. Are you doing *all but only* what God designed you to do? Before God, think about the things that give you joy and that delight others. Consider these your blessed boundaries and allow them to guide you as you seek His direction on a daily basis and strive to properly order your priorities.

CHAPTER FOUR

Proper Priorities
Produce Peace

"Heav'n above is softer blue,
Earth around is sweeter green!
Something lives in every hue
Christ-less eyes have never seen:
Birds with gladder songs o'er-flow,
Flow'rs with deeper beauties shine,
Since I know, as now I know, I am His, and He is mine."
George W. Robinson

Once you learn the basics of God's goal and purpose for your life, identify your life calling, and understand how your life work enables the call, you must move on to the next step: discerning daily direction. Life is an accumulation of days filled with hours and moments of choices. Those daily and momentary choices determine the effectiveness of a life; thus it behooves us to regularly, soberly, and sincerely seek to know the boundaries of the will of God.

To know God's will requires spending time with Him,

enough time to quiet the heart, focus the thoughts, share concerns and questions and, most importantly, time to listen and discern direction. Jesus knew that the secret to successfully completing His mission in life entailed focusing every energy on His Father's priorities and not allowing anything else to sidetrack Him, even the expectations of the people around Him. To that end, He properly ordered His priorities and took direction from God alone. He says in John 6:38, "For I have come down from heaven, not to do my own will but the will of him who sent me."

Mark gives us an example of this discipline in his first chapter. In verse 35 he records that Jesus rose early, "while it was still dark," and went away for a time of solitude and prayer. The disciples soon came to find him because "everyone is looking for you." (1:37b) To that, I would likely respond by ending my prayers and returning immediately to see to the needs of the people, but not Christ. He knew the importance of spending time alone with God, and what is more, He had orders to move on to another place. In verse 38, we read, "And he said to them, 'Let us go on to the next towns, that I may preach there also, for that is why I came out'."

Luke records a similar instance in 4:42-44, "And when it was day, he departed and went into a desolate place. And the people sought him and came to him, and would have kept him from leaving them, but he said to them, 'I must preach the good news of the kingdom of God to the other towns as well; for I was sent for this purpose.' And he was preaching in the synagogues of Judea." Rather than responding quickly to the pressing need, Christ paused and listened to the greater priority: the call of His Father to keep moving.

His private time with the Father prepared Christ for the public ministry He faced each day. The people could wait; approaching ministry without the direction and blessing of the Father was unthinkable. Would that we learned from His example that our most important preparation occurs in stillness and solitude! Effectiveness in ministry is proportional to our time alone with God. We are not likely to have the same amount of time to spend with Him every day, but we cannot experience God's blessings without making time with Him our highest priority on a consistent basis.

God brought this lesson home to me during the first year I served as a resident assistant at Messiah. At one point I felt guilty about the amount of time I spent by myself and in devotional time with the Lord. In order to truly give myself in ministry to the young women on "my floor," I felt I should maintain instant accessibility. In my pride, it seemed my effectiveness as a mentor depended on *my* availability and wisdom.

As I pondered this in prayer one morning, the Lord reminded me clearly that the only things of lasting value I offer others are those applications of truths I receive from Him. The fruit of the Spirit flows forth to others in words of kindness and love, expressions of joy and gentleness, acts of self-control and faith. But, these only exist in my life when I spend time with God and soak in the truths of His Word. True wisdom is based on Scripture and comes most readily to mind after I study, memorize and meditate upon it. I am learning to pray that only what God inspires will pierce the hearts and capture the minds of those with whom I share, and that anything of me will pass quickly through their minds and not linger in their imagination.

TIMING IS EVERYTHING

Because Jesus spent time with His Father regularly and measured His steps by His Father's will, He had an impeccable sense of timing. In Luke 4:41, Jesus commands the demons not to identify Him because He knew the time for that revelation was not at hand. After feeding the 5,000, John records Jesus' response to the people, "Perceiving then that they were about to come and take him by force to make him king, Jesus withdrew again to the mountain by himself." (John 6:15) Jesus knew He still had things to accomplish before fulfilling, in part, the wishes of the people. Had He not sought direction from above, perhaps the energy and purpose of those who wanted to prematurely exalt Him and pledge their allegiance would have swayed Him. But, the timing was not right; He knew the order of God's priorities differed from that of the people.When I first began working for a ministry, I longed to carry over the vision for discipleship God gave me at Messiah. I spent much time thinking about ways to encourage and mentor the other young women serving at the offices in Indianapolis and the headquarters in Chicago. At one point, I compiled my ideas in a notebook and presented them to the president of the ministry, sure that he only needed to see the plan in order to give me the go ahead to put it into action. But that did not happen. The notebook got buried in a pile on his desk, and I left for home thinking my time with this ministry was over.

A couple years later, during my first spring in Dallas, the Lord gave me the vision for Advanced EXCEL. After writing out a proposal, I sent the plans, with my boss' blessing, to our president, and this time I received an affirming response. However, the timing just did not seem right. Like an unfinished puzzle, the pieces were not all in place and another vision idled. Later in the year however, as my family made plans to move to Texas, I began developing courses and recruiting instructors and students. And, a year after drafting the initial outline of the program our first group of 12 met, and the vision sputtered to life.

Then in 1998, when we began splitting our time between Dallas and Chicago, the timing ripened for the other vision: discipling young women in the ministry. Since my father recruited, trained, and generally supervised the student staff, he established an accountability structure for those living on the premises at the headquarters. He assigned me the task of encouraging and nurturing leaders in each of the women's housing units who in turn, mentored the others in their home or apartment.

Since then, I have had the privilege of watching both visions mature. Once God's timing arrived, His plans moved forward without a struggle. The continuity of both programs bears witness to the reality that He is fully capable of accomplishing His work in His time and impacting the lives He intended to impact with these programs since the beginning of time. My biggest challenge is learning to wait on Him and trust His sense of timing.

Working with hundreds of girls and young women, mothers and couples who attend the various conferences and events at the hotel in Dallas also serves to remind me to wait on the Lord. Many arrive wearing needs on their faces and others walk through the doors with masks firmly fixed. My father wisely reminds us, "There's a melodrama behind every smiling face." And we have seen many over the years.

At first, I spent a lot of energy teaching, sharing, imploring, coaxing and even pleading for people to surrender their hurts and accept God's forgiveness and peace. I have learned though, that the most effective thing I can do is pray for the needs I see and hear. I am powerless to change another's heart and give them a desire for righteousness. If a person resists the wooing of God's Holy Spirit to change, why should I expect them to respond to my reasoning? I have had to learn to wait on God's timing and make prayer my priority, just as Christ did.

PEACE IN EVERY CIRCUMSTANCE

Because Christ relied upon and trusted in the will of the Father, He experienced peace in the midst of varying circumstances. Indeed, peace is a good indicator of trust: little trust equals little peace while great trust enables great peace.

I found it amazing, as I studied each of the gospels, to see that Jesus did not rush. Peace permeated His work. He remained calm whether speaking to thousands or healing one person, addressing important leaders or quieting a storm.

Christ was even at peace at the end of His life. We see Him in Luke 22 and 23 handle a variety of situations without anxiety. Though hours away from agony, He prepares for and observes the Passover with the disciples, even explaining his coming betrayal in a non-emotional way. He settles the dispute regarding the marks of greatness in the midst of their meal without losing His temper. When He walks to Gethsemane, He teaches along the way, sharing some of the most beautiful passages in all of Scripture about the importance of simply abiding in Him and the will of His Father.

We see him praying in the garden, overwhelmed by the burden He faces, yet not out of control; distraught, but not beside Himself. He faces Judas' betrayal, Peter's denial, the disciples' desertion, the trial and torture, and the sentencing all without exploding in anger or rage. He stumbles down the Via Dolorosa in chapter 23 in intense pain, yet with enough compassion to warn the daughters of Jerusalem not to weep for Him, but for themselves and their children. At the cross we see Him in agony, far beyond what we can imagine, and yet he does not lash out at His tormentors. Though He cries out in anguish, "My God, my God, why hast Thou forsaken me?" He trusts the Father to the very last, even at the terrible moment when God turns His face from the sin covering His beloved Son.

Peace was one of the important legacies He left behind, a challenge to his followers through the ages. "Peace I leave with you; my peace I give to you. Not as the world gives do I give to you. Let not your hearts be troubled, neither let them be afraid." (John 14:27) The level of peace we enjoy reflects the degree of our trust in God. When I keep my eyes fixed on Him, I have peace. When I look at things around me instead, anxiety overwhelms me. I believe one of the greatest lessons of the Christian life is to focus so clearly on God and to know His priorities so fully, that peace permeates my life because nothing shakes my trust in Him. Circumstances have little to do with mental outlook when we are confidently doing the right things.

MAKING TIME A PRIORITY

The story of Mary and Martha in Luke 10 challenges me, because Mary illustrates the kind of person I want to be and Martha embodies the kind of person I tend to be. These two demonstrate correct and incorrect priorities. One recognizes the importance of time with Jesus, and one allows her eyes to go from Him to the list of things to do without taking time to just enjoy the Lord's presence in her home and in her life. The story is familiar: Jesus comes to the home of these sisters and their brother, Lazarus, for a visit. Mary, to Martha's chagrin, sits at Jesus' feet and listens to His teaching rather than helping to prepare the meal. Martha's responsibilities in hosting this dinner fluster her to the point of distraction, and she attempts to boss Jesus and shame her sister into coming to help her in the kitchen.

Jesus tells Martha, "... you are anxious and troubled about many things, but one thing is necessary. Mary has chosen the good portion, which will not be taken away from her." (Luke 10:41-42) Peace permeated Christ's life because He spent time at His Father's feet, and He knew that Martha would experience the same peace He – and Mary – knew, if she would only take the time to communicate with Him. Jesus sets her priorities straight and shows us what demonstrates love to Him: quality time. Of course, other things show love to Christ as well, but if we analyze the way He spent the days of His earthly ministry, we see that He greatly valued focused time with others.

Several years ago our family read a book that forever changed the ways in which we interact. Entitled <u>The Five Love Languages</u>, the authors of this book describe how different things say, "I love you" to different people. For some, spending time together communicating shows love; for others, physical affection demonstrates care and concern. Some respond to gifts, and some like to serve their loved ones to show how much they mean to them. The final group looks for and gives words of praise to highlight their love for others. We all appreciate giving and receiving love in a variety of ways, but for most of us, one way means more than the others.

Learning to recognize each other's love languages helped us to communicate love and affirmation much better. For example, my mother's primary love language is quality time, which for her means time with just our immediate family spent talking together with little or no outside distraction. Lingering around the table to talk after finishing a meal nourishes her more than the food. No one else in the family has this particular love language, and prior to reading the book, it continually frustrated us that Mom's drive for time together never seemed satisfied. After a night of eating pizza and watching a video, she would lament that we just did not spend enough time as a family. That caused the rest of us to look at each other with raised eyebrows and an expression that said, "What have we done for the last two hours?!"

After reading the book, we realized that Mom's definition of quality time differed from the rest of ours. We felt like we had spent quality time together just by sitting in the same room enjoying a movie. But, that did not spell love to Mother. For an activity to equal quality time to her, it had to involve verbal communication. So, in order to demonstrate our love for her, we learned to reorganize our priorities and restructure our time together to include meaningful, unhurried conversation. The fact that she was different did not mean that she needed to change. It meant that the rest of us needed to learn to show love in a way that she could really receive and by which she felt affirmed.

In the same way, if the Lord wants quality time with us and we know that demonstrates love to Him, we should structure our days to make that our number one priority. That is not to say that He needs our love – He needs nothing from us. But He offers Himself in relationship to us and it behooves us to love Him in the ways He clearly instructs us in Scripture. He also delights in our service, our gifts, our verbal affirmation and in the ways we touch others in His name, but it is in giving Him our time that we show our true surrender to His love.

One of my favorite passages in the Psalms highlights this important truth. God speaks in Psalm 50, verse 7 and following, saying, "For every beast of the forest is mine, the cattle on a thousand hills. I know all the birds of the hills, and all that moves in the field is mine. If I were hungry, I would not tell you, for the world and its fullness are mine. Do I eat the flesh of bulls or drink the blood of goats?"

God sets the stage here to tell the Israelites – and us – what really demonstrates love and commitment to Him. Verses 14 and 15 continue, "Offer to God a sacrifice of thanksgiving, and perform your vows to the Most High, and call upon me in the day of trouble; I will deliver you, and you shall glorify me." Our thanksgiving, worship and acknowledgment of need glorify the Most High God. He values these offerings of the heart, not the sacrifices and burnt offerings of flesh.

THE VALUE OF REST

I tend to want to show my love to God through the things I *do*. This is more comfortable for me because I remain in control. Trying to do more than I have physical strength for contributed greatly to my exhaustion, and I am learning now that the Lord wants the priceless gift of my heart first, rather than the feeble offerings of my hands. To give Him my heart takes time, time spent alone with Him in solitude and prayer. In order to have energy for time with Him, I must balance my desire to work with my need to rest. Even in this area, Jesus sets the example.

In addition to spending time with His Heavenly Father, Jesus made time for rest a priority for Himself and the disciples. Rest did not necessarily mean sleep or recreation in the ways we might think of today. For Christ, time for rest included time with the Father along with fishing with his disciples and walking the roads of Galilee. In Matthew 14:22-23, after a long day of ministry, Jesus sends the disciples on their way in a boat and then goes back to send the people home. Verse 23 records, "And after he had dismissed the crowds, he went up on the mountain by himself to pray. When evening came, he was there alone." Prayer is an essential part of reviving from as well as preparing for ministry, and this time restored Him before He rejoined the disciples.

In Mark 6:30, the disciples return from teaching and ministering in other places. Jesus listens to their accounts and gives them time to process their experiences, and then in verse 31 He says, "Come away by yourselves to a desolate place and rest a while.' For many were coming and going, and they had no leisure even to eat."

Getting away for rest and time alone was a practice, not just an exceptional part of Jesus' schedule. "When Jesus had spoken these words, he went out with his disciples across the Kidron Valley, where there was a garden, which he and his disciples entered. Now Judas, who betrayed him, also knew the place, *for Jesus often met there* with his disciples." (John 18:1-2, emphasis mine)

Christ realized what I often fail to, that sometimes rest is more important than continual, non-stop ministry to the multitudes. Indeed, the rest helps to preserve me so that I live to minister another day.

The symptoms I have experienced in the last few years remind me daily of this truth. I tried to push myself beyond my God-given boundaries of physical and emotional strength and ended up hindering rather than helping any kind of ministry to others. Knowing one's limits and respecting them is critical for anyone who desires to give their life in service to God. It is impossible to keep the pace of a 100-yard sprint throughout a 26-mile marathon.

God calls us to a lifetime of furthering His kingdom and He does not intend for us to burn out at the beginning. When I began "full-time Christian ministry" after college, a desire to use time efficiently for the sake of the kingdom largely motivated my service. I felt compelled to sprint and equated a slow pace with failure. When God allowed my ability to *do* to be taken away for a time, I floundered, wondering what value my life held if I could not produce visible results at the end of each day.

During that time, I reflected on the pace of life described in the gospels, as well as throughout the Scriptures. Our spiritual forefathers led fairly slow-paced lives compared to ours, with all of our modern tools for convenience and speed. We differ from them like the Concorde differs from the snail. Were Jesus consumed with efficiency, He could have come in our day and used all the resources of radio and the Internet to send His message to the four corners of the earth, airplanes to carry Him around the globe, speaker systems to amplify His voice to millions. He could have used a handheld computer to organize His schedule and cell phones to keep tabs on the disciples at all times.

Christ did not do this. The Father sent Him at the perfect time; to a slow-moving culture without the resources or conveniences we take for granted. In this time where most people walked from place to place and a good set of lungs were one's only hope for amplification, where a "long trip" meant sailing across the Sea of Galilee, He came and used His time effectively. He accomplished everything the Father gave Him to do with the simple resources at His disposal. God loved Him perfectly because He obeyed His will with the resources He had. We can learn much from His example. Yes, we can multiply our time and energies through modern resources, but that should allow us *more* time to rest, pray and reflect on God's will rather than feeling like we have less time.

THE IMPORTANCE OF BALANCE – EVEN AT THE END

Jesus knew the proper balance between work and rest. Even at the end of His life, He did not work night and day. He understood that rest is an integral part of God's design, an absolutely essential priority for every human being. God created daytime for work and nighttime for rest, and resisting that concept only serves to weaken the body and limit our effectiveness.

Jesus understood this principle, though if a sense of urgency about needing to complete tasks attempted to consume anyone, surely it would have been Him. His reason for living was the most critical any man will ever face. Yet, just days before his death, Luke records Him teaching during the day in the temple and spending the evenings on the Mount of Olives (Luke 21:37-38). He rose early to teach, but He still took time to come apart at night. I would expect Christ to throw caution to the wind and work day and night because He knew the time was so short. Instead, He continued to pace Himself as He prepared to endure the betrayal and crucifixion.

Because Christ kept His priorities in order throughout His life, He was able to say at the end of it, "It is finished" (John 19:30). Without the benefits of our modern technology or even an "average" life span, this Man changed the course of human history and altered the destiny of mankind forever. His impact was measured by His ability to keep His priorities in order: He spent time with His Father and took His direction only from Him. He worked diligently and did not begrudge the time needed to rest and simply *be*. He knew His boundaries and found blessing within them. In doing so, He lived each day with peace in His spirit, joy in His eyes, and unstoppable love in His heart.

CHAPTER FIVE

Putting Prayer in its Proper Place – First

"Speak, Lord, in the stillness while I wait on Thee;
Hushed my heart to listen in expectancy.
Fill me with the knowledge of Thy glorious will;
All Thine own good pleasure in Thy child fulfill."
E. May Grimes

I struggle with prayer. Talking to an invisible force seems foolish if you pause to think about it. You cannot see someone listening or responding when you pray. If you suddenly come upon a person in prayer, talking aloud or just moving their lips silently, it appears sense has become a distant friend, really distant.

Prayer also seems like a waste of time for a doer. The spirit of a go-getter whispers, "Why sit around talking about a problem? Get busy solving it!" Yet over and over in Scripture God commands us – not just encourages or challenges – commands us, to pray. I Thessalonians 5:17 says, "Pray without ceasing." James 5:16 instructs, "Therefore, confess your sins to one another and pray for one another, that you may be healed. The prayer of a righteous person has great power as it is working." Paul writes in Philippians 4:6, "Do not be anxious about anything, but in everything by prayer and supplication with thanksgiving let your requests be made known to God."

In Chapter Four we looked at the priorities Christ established for His life and prayer topped the list. In this chapter, we will look more closely at Christ's example as well as hindrances and motivations to prayer. By making prayer His highest priority, Jesus set the standard for all who desire to follow in His footsteps. Luke records a story with this beginning, "And He (Christ) told them a parable to the effect that they ought always to pray and not lose heart." (18:1) He modeled obedience to the command to pray, as well as teaching those around Him the boundaries of where, how, when, what and why to pray.

THE LOGISTICS OF PRAYER - WHERE

In Matthew 5 starting in verse 5, Christ instructs His followers to pray in secret instead of making a pretentious show in front of others, like the religious leaders of the day. Jesus reminds them that the Heavenly Father sees, even the secret, and openly rewards those who pray. Although we know we can pray in any place and at any time, by emphasizing personal, private prayer, Jesus points us to the foundation for all other prayer. In the introduction to his book, <u>Developing Your Secret Closet of Prayer</u>, Richard Burr makes the statement, "My persuasion is this: one's spiritual life will never rise above the practice of one's private prayer life."

Christ prayed with His disciples; He taught them to pray by demonstrating. But His life reflected such rich spiritual significance because even the Son of God made private time with His Father a priority. He began His days with prayer: "And rising very early in the morning, while it was still dark, he departed and went out to a desolate place, and there he prayed." (Mark 1:35) At the end of a long day, He took time to pray: "And after he had dismissed the crowds, he went up on the mountain by himself to pray. When evening came, he was there alone." (Matthew 14:23) Before making big decisions, he made time to commune with His Father: "In these days he went out to the mountain to pray, and all night he continued in prayer to God. And when day came, he called his disciples and chose from them twelve, whom he named apostles." (Luke 6:12-13) When the time came for His greatest testing, He sought the Father alone: "Then Jesus went with them to a place called Gethsemane, and he said to his disciples, 'Sit here, while I go over there and pray'." (Matthew 26:36)

Personal, private prayer time is an important answer to the question of where we pray. A significant prayer life begins within the boundaries of our private lives. If we do not have significant prayer time alone, we are unlikely to have it with others.

THE LOGISTICS OF PRAYER - HOW

After instructing the disciples to pray in secret, Jesus addresses the "how" of prayer by challenging them to pray humbly and simply: "And when you pray, do not heap up empty phrases as the Gentiles do, for they think that they will be heard for their many words." (Matthew 6:7) The heathen came to God with their list of wants and expectations. Jesus wanted the disciples to understand that prayer is much more than asking. We only communicate when we listen as well as speak, and real prayer involves hearing from God as well as telling Him our needs and wants. Burr says, "The essence of prayer is not what I can get from God. Prayer is to be an intimate and personal relationship with our living God in which the believer comes to want only what God wants for him, nothing more and nothing less." (p.5)

God has established the boundaries of His instruction to us by His written word. I have found the easiest way to "listen" to God to be to approach my Scripture reading each day with specific requests in mind or written down. Then, I ask the Holy Spirit to help me as I read slowly and meditate, looking for the answers. They may not come the first day. And, the requests may be ones I make more than once; such as asking the Lord to draw unsaved loved ones to Himself. I have also found that sometimes the Lord will "speak to me" when the Holy Spirit brings a memorized portion of Scripture to mind while I am thinking or praying about a particular request. While certainly not the only way, this approach has helped to deepen my sense of communication with God and further develop my love for His Word.

WHAT TO PRAY

Continuing in Matthew 6, Christ demonstrates the "what" of prayer by providing an outline:

"After this manner therefore pray ye:
Our Father which art in heaven, Hallowed be Thy name.
Thy kingdom come.
Thy will be done in earth, as it is in heaven.
Give us this day our daily bread.
And forgive us our debts, as we forgive our debtors.
And lead us not into temptation, but deliver us from evil:
For Thine is the kingdom, and the power, and the glory,
forever. Amen." (KJV)

This outline includes all the important elements of prayer. It begins with praise and acknowledgement of God's sovereign place in heaven. It is so important to begin prayer by remembering who God is, because meditating on Him also reminds us of who we are in comparison. When we stop to contemplate His holiness and majesty we are much less likely to barge into the heavenly throne room and carelessly toss our requests at our Heavenly Father. Pausing to praise His attributes should slow us down and bring us into His presence with a proper sense of awe and wonder at His graciousness to permit our entrance at all.

The second part of this prayer reminds us to consider God's will in the events of our lives, as well as the happenings of the world. We are much better off beseeching Him to do His perfect work in and through us for the glory of His name than bringing Him a laundry list of items designed to bring comfort and glory to ourselves.

WHY PRAY?

After remembering the holiness of God and the all-consuming importance of His will, Jesus instructs us to lay our personal requests at the Father's feet. God wants to provide for the needs of His people, but He also wants us to depend on Him and realize that His mercy supplies our need, not our hard work. While we can certainly ponder these things outside of the prayer closet, we are probably much more likely to think on them in this quiet place, away from the distractions that fill our busy lives.

Next, we need God's grace to walk in forgiveness and His protection from the temptations that surround us. Jesus' instruction to pray for deliverance from temptation and evil on a daily basis should motivate us to do so. If the Son of God takes sin and the enemy of our souls seriously, so should we. Jesus closes this model prayer with another reminder that God alone deserves glory, honor and praise, both in this world and in the reality beyond time and space.

This kind of prayer should put many things in perspective for us. It honors and glorifies God alone and acknowledges Him as the Source of all we need, the answer to every question. Jesus understood a fact that we, who like to think ourselves self-sufficient, often overlook. When we see a need, we want to jump in immediately and start working the problem until we find an acceptable solution. Jesus never did that because He knew that the answer to greater needs is greater prayer, not harder work. This is "why" we pray. His words in Matthew 9:37-38 perhaps articulate this better than any other passage. After teaching, preaching and healing the people, their obvious needs moved Him to compassion. I would expect Him to keep working to meet them Himself, or perhaps goad the disciples on to a faster pace. Instead He says, "The harvest is plentiful, but the laborers are few; therefore pray earnestly to the Lord of the harvest to send out laborers into his harvest."

Pray? He tells them to pray rather than just work harder? This is a godly boundary we often ignore or reject. For some, this is a foolish and intolerable command. Foolish, because it appears that nothing will get done if we do not do it ourselves. Who will heal the sick? Who will teach the ignorant? Who will enlighten the seekers? And, intolerable because we would rather do anything in the face of a challenge but wait on God, or anyone else, for direction. John Piper writes, "To wait! That means to pause and soberly consider our own inadequacy and the Lord's all sufficiency, and to seek counsel and help from the Lord, and to hope in Him." (Desiring God, pg. 146) I enjoy waiting about as much as sitting in the shade, slapping mosquitoes. The Lord's Prayer in Matthew 6 is a powerful tool for conquering impatience and self-sufficiency.

WHEN TO PRAY

Jesus had many answers for the multitudes and much wisdom to impart to the disciples, but even the godliest man to ever walk the planet realized that, for the human, any real power or sufficiency exists only in the Father. And so, in addition to making prayer His top priority, Jesus taught them saying, "Therefore I tell you, whatever you ask in prayer, believe that you have received it, and it will be yours." (Mark 11:24) Jesus knew the secret: prayer IS the work. This is the "when:" prayer must precede the doing if the doing is to succeed.

Jesus displayed His understanding of this principle and His dependence on the Father in countless ways. One of my favorites is when He fed the multitudes. Mark describes the scene like this:

"In those days, when again a great crowd had gathered, and they had nothing to eat, he called his disciples to him and said to them, 'I have compassion on the crowd, because they have been with me now three days and have nothing to eat. And if I send them away hungry to their homes, they will faint on the way. And some of them have come from far away.'

And his disciples answered him, 'How can one feed these people with bread here in this desolate place?'

And he asked them, 'How many loaves do you have?' They said, 'Seven.'

And he directed the crowd to sit down on the ground. And he took the seven loaves, and *having given thanks*, he broke them and gave them to his disciples to set before the people; and they set them before the crowd. And they had a few small fish. And *having blessed them*, he said that these also should be set before them. And they ate and were satisfied. And they took up the broken pieces left over, seven baskets full." (chapter 8:1-8, emphasis mine)

Overwhelming need stretched out before Christ in the form of thousands of hungry followers. They came to Him for spiritual food, but He longed to meet their physical needs as well. He asked the disciples about their resources and a quick count showed them sadly lacking. So, He took what they had and offered it first to the Father. He prayed, asking for blessing and giving God thanks, and then the miracle occurred. It was the Father who fed the thousands, in response to Jesus' request for His blessing. In this instance, He answered promptly, abundantly, and in a way that visibly glorified Him and His Son.

And, the Father meets the needs before us when we ask Him to intervene on our behalf. "God is not looking for people to work for Him, so much as He is looking for people who will let Him work for them." (John Piper, <u>Desiring God</u>, p.146) Too often I forget to offer my resources to the Father and wear out because alone, I am as limited as the disciples with only a few measly fish for the multitudes. I look at the impossible situation facing me and take inventory of my resources. Far too often, I see something, albeit small, in my hands and immediately set to work to meet the need with what I have. My resources do not go far, nor do they last long. I forget the Psalmist's instruction in Psalm 57:2, "I will cry unto God most high; unto *God that performeth* all things for me." (KJV)

I began learning the importance of making prayer a priority during the summers I spent on the mission field as a teenager. It was the policy and practice of the mission group to assign people to pray throughout the daily work hours. Each member of the team spent an hour every few days lifting the needs of the team to the Lord, praying for protection, asking for wisdom for our leaders and blessing on our work. The hours I spent in the "prayer closet" are hallowed in my memory. In these times, I became vividly aware that our work depended, absolutely and completely, upon the benevolence and provision of God. Without Him, we were helpless to do anything of lasting value.

At times we implement a similar prayer rotation in Dallas based on the needs of those attending our conferences. We have found that when we pray, we see greater results, not just in our guests, but also in our staff. Everyone has to work a little harder when we do this because we feel the loss of hands on those busy days, yet we cannot ignore the results. Not surprisingly, God moves when we make prayer a priority!

During one eight-week conference, a student stubbornly struggled. She resisted the truth and told anyone who would listen that she did not belong to Christ and had no intention of accepting His provision for her salvation. Speakers took extra time to encourage her and answer her questions, but for seven long weeks she resisted every appeal to receive Christ. As the last week rolled around, the leadership team began to fast and pray for her. We took turns praying from the beginning of the day through the end of the evening session. We cried out to God, jealous for her soul and keenly aware of our inability to change her heart. After about two and a half days, she came to her team leader, and in tears, proclaimed her need of Christ and desire to receive His saving grace for herself. We rejoiced for her, but also recognized that God had accomplished a miracle through prayer.

HINDRANCES TO PRAYER

Yes, it is God that does the work when we cry out to Him. Who better to meet needs than the One who fashioned the universe, set the stars in place, knits bones together in the womb, watches the sparrows, and stores bottles of tears? E.M. Bounds once said, "That man cannot possibly be called a Christian, who does not pray." (The Necessity of Prayer, p.40) When I act before praying, I live like an atheist. Bounds also wrote, "We simply cannot talk to God, strongly, intimately, and confidently unless we are living for him, faithfully and truly." (p.49) Let's look at some common reasons we do not follow Christ's example and make prayer our top priority.

Self – sufficiency

If we are honest, neglecting – or refusing – to pray indicates a heart of pride and self-sufficiency, thinking we can "go it alone" without God's help. The atheist does this intentionally by deluding himself with the thought that the infinitely complex universe somehow appeared and evolved by chance. Believers should know better: we believe God exists and trust Him to provide eternal security through the sacrifice of Christ. However, when we neglect prayer, we say by our actions that the God we trust for eternity is not needed for the decisions we make in time, the daily tasks, challenges, problems, and relationships that fill our lives.

This is foolishness, and yet I know I fall prey to the mirage of self-sufficiency on a regular basis. How many mornings do I choose sleep over a quiet hour in the prayer closet because I think the rest more important than time with the Lord? How many meetings do I plunge into throughout the day without asking God to direct my thinking, my conversation and my attitudes? How many times do I leave the driveway without asking the Lord for protection on the roads because I trust in my own ability rather than His sovereignty? How many nights do I turn out the light and allow the events of the day to replay in my mind rather than leaving them at the foot of the throne? In all these ways and many more I take God's presence in my life for granted and fancy myself in control.

Impatience

Lack of prayer also demonstrates an impatient heart, one unwilling to wait on an answer that seems delayed by my timetable. King Saul demonstrated this kind of impatience in I Samuel 13 when he proceeded with the sacrifice because Samuel did not appear on the scene when Saul expected him. Had he stopped to pray rather than acting impetuously, perhaps he would have garnered the patience and grace to keep waiting. By moving ahead of God and offering the sacrifice himself, he lost the favor of both God and Samuel.

Whether intentional or not, my works without prayer loudly proclaim my independence and lack of trust in God. He is not moving at my speed or according to my plan, so I decide to bypass prayer and "get on with the show." This inevitably leads me away from God's will for my life and hinders the work He seeks to accomplish through me. "When I forfeit my time of solitude with the Master, the embers of my heart grow cool and my 'first love' becomes a memory of the past rather than the reality of the present." (Richard Burr, <u>Developing Your Secret Closet of Prayer</u>, p.153) Years ago I began to pray that the Lord would let me fall apart quickly whenever I walked away from Him in order to minimize the damage to my life and others by my laziness and impatience. God seems to delight in answering this prayer because He never allows me to stray far.

Bitterness

Unforgiveness and bitterness also hinder prayer. Jesus said, "For if you forgive others their trespasses, your heavenly Father will also forgive you, but if you do not forgive others their trespasses, neither will your Father forgive your trespasses." (Matthew 6:14 – 15) We cannot expect to see bold answers when we know we are impertinently praying while living in direct disobedience to this command. God will not honor our prayers while we hold bitterness and unforgiveness toward others in our hearts. This is so important that we will deal with it more thoroughly in Chapter Ten.

THE GIFT OF REPENTANCE

So, in order to pray with the effectiveness of Christ, it is critical that I bring any known sin, be it self-sufficiency, impatience or bitterness, and leave it at the foot of the cross. I may also need to ask the Holy Spirit to show me my heart and give me the gift of repentance if I feel distant from God but cannot think of specific sins. J. Edwin Orr wrote, "It is to the Holy Spirit that the Christian must look if he is to find a measure of revival for his searching soul. Spiritual blessing for believers is dependent on a cleansing, which in turn depends upon confession that is dependent on conviction; and conviction comes from a searching of heart by God's own Spirit." (as quoted by Richard Burr, p.126)

Not only is prayer a necessary *means* of repenting of sin and making my heart right with the Heavenly Father, the process of prayer *causes* repentance as I meditate in God's presence on who He is and who I am in comparison. Bounds also said, "Prayer produces cleanliness of heart and purity of life." (The Necessity of Prayer, p.48) This is true, because as we pray, our sensitivity to the Holy Spirit grows. We will probably go through cycles of cleansing the soul, unpleasant, but necessary in order to purify the mind, will, and emotions and tear down walls of sin that separate us from God, with or without our awareness.

My first cycle of cleansing occurred when I moved to Indianapolis. In Ephesians 4:26-27, Paul warns, "Be angry and do not sin; do not let the sun go down on your anger, and give no opportunity to the devil." During those months, I learned of Satan's ability to build strongholds in my soul, places he camps when my unconfessed sin leaves openings. Left uncontested, Satan uses these places in my mind, will and emotions to capitalize on my sin and weave His lies into my perspective on life, attitudes toward others, and relationship with God.

To regain freedom, I learned to confess my sins to God, as specifically as possible, and ask Him to take back the places in my life I unwittingly surrendered to the enemy. I spent hours in prayer confessing all the sin I could think of, mostly the effects of negative influences in movies, music, and books that distracted me from the truths of God's Word. I asked the Holy Spirit to bring any and all things to mind that were keeping me from enjoying an unhindered relationship with the Lord and thus spent hours on my knees alone in my room. The process humbled me, because I did not realize how much had accumulated over the years. But as I prayed and the Lord cleaned the house of my heart, new-found freedom and joy arose. Scripture came alive like never before, not just as I read the Bible, but also in the hymns I sang since many of them are based on Biblical principles.

In the years since the Fall of 1993, I have walked through many more cycles of cleansing. One day recently, after a visit to my chiropractor, who occasionally doubles as a counselor, I left frustrated. I stifled the tears until I reached the car, started the engine and pulled onto the highway, but then they flowed freely. He had put his finger right on an area of spiritual weakness and after several months of similar experiences in his office, I felt I had heard enough.

"Lord," I complained, "why don't you pick on someone else for a change? Why do you keep pushing me, uncovering failures and spotlighting 'small' sins? Can't you just leave me alone to recover my health in peace? Why must I deal with these issues on top of the unpleasantness of my illness?"

At that moment I heard the quiet voice of the Holy Spirit asking, "Lauren, what do you pray for almost every day?"

"What do you mean, what do I pray for?" I snapped back.

Immediately the verses I often breezed through while my mind ran ahead to the next request came to mind. "Search me, O God, and know my heart! Try me and know my thoughts! And see if there be any grievous way in me, and lead me in the way everlasting!" (Psalm 139: 23 – 24)

"Oh, Lord," I thought, "*those* verses. I suppose you really take me seriously, don't You? Do you mean this inquisition is an answer to my prayers? You are looking for *any* grievous thing to expose and heal when I confess it as sin?"

I spent the rest of the ride home confessing my particular sin, along with the pride of not wanting God to point out the blind spots in my life. Then I asked Him to take back the room these sins made in my heart for Satan and his lies. This event prompted me to reconsider Scriptures I regularly prayed to determine if other current circumstances could be answers in disguise. As I began to take inventory, I realized that God was using my illness to bring to fruition years of petitioning Him to work in my life. We'll explore these prayers and their implications in the next chapter.

BUILDING TRUST

Once we repent of any known sin, we can focus on building what is perhaps the most necessary quality for effective prayer: trust that God is who He says He is. Jesus successfully modeled prayer because He, more than anyone else, understood the depth of His Father's faithfulness. Trusting God's heart came second nature to Christ for He carefully nurtured that relationship with His time and energy, making it His top priority in life.

It is difficult to pray if we do not trust the One to whom we pray, just like it is difficult to love without a foundation of trust. At one point in my illness I realized that the root of some of my problems was lack of trust in God that resulted from blaming Him for painful events in my life. This lack of trust gave Satan fertile ground for sowing seeds of additional pain, fear, and anxiety that drew me further from my Source of healing. Because I did not trust God completely, it was hard to turn to Him when these negative emotions threatened to consume me.

Once I admitted to myself and to the Lord that I was really upset with *Him*, I was able to confess my sin and begin the healing process. Like Job, I had to come to the realization that God owes me no explanation for the events He allows in my life. He reveals His character through Scripture and that is the only "defense" He provides for why He does what He does. When I recognized this, Scripture came alive in new ways and I regained my ability to pray with the Psalmist passages like Psalm 62:5-8, "For God alone, O my soul, wait in silence, for my hope is from him.

He only is my rock and my salvation, my fortress; I shall not be shaken. On God rests my salvation and my glory; my mighty rock, my refuge is God. Trust in him at all times, O people; pour out your heart before him; God is a refuge for us. Selah."

Christ had this type of ultimate faith in His Father. He understood that living within His boundaries meant waiting on God and looking to Him to answer every prayer. He depended on God, not on His human strength, and this trust guided Him through the opposition He faced in His earthly life and ministry. Though Christ knew He came to save the world, He believed in the Father and took refuge in their relationship. He made fellowship with God in the morning, at night, and throughout the day His number one priority. And thus, He set the perfect example for us to follow.

CHAPTER SIX

Using Scripture
to Pray Effectively

"Speak, O blessed Master, in this quiet hour;
Let me see Thy face, Lord, feel Thy touch of power.
For the words Thou speakest, they are life indeed;
Living bread from heaven, now my spirit feed."
E. May Grimes

*I*f I truly desire to follow Christ's example and make pursuing God through the means of prayer the top priority of my life, then I need to rearrange my daily schedule. This begins with disciplining myself to go to bed early enough that rising before the rush of morning activities begins is not impossible. I may need to adjust my morning routine in order to allow for uninterrupted time in my private prayer closet. I must try to discipline myself to pray throughout the day as I move from activity to activity so that I include the Lord in all that I do. And, I can ask the Holy Spirit to prompt me to pray when I get busy and forget along the way.

In addition to reorganizing my time, I should make every

effort to pray within the boundaries of God's will. I can pray according to biblical principles as I study and meditate on His Word. Another way to ensure I pray in accordance with God's will is to incorporate Scripture, His perfect revealed will, into my daily prayers.

Prior to learning to pray Scripture, I found my prayers often seemed trite. I read through a list asking simple things such as "God please bless Mom, Dad, Julianne, Jamie, Adam, Amy, Grandmother, Lydia, Chloe, Christian, Ava, etc." While not a bad place to start, this approach lacks depth. God certainly desires to hear words straight from my heart to His, but using His own words as a springboard for prayer has deepened my understanding of the Bible as well as added significance to what I ask for myself and others. "The Word and prayer are inseparable. When one engages in prayer without the Word it can lead to mysticism; when the Word is used without prayer it can lead to legalism, intellectualism and coldness of heart." (Richard Burr, Developing Your Secret Closet of Prayer, p.80)

Burr goes on to say, "Engaging in Scripture praying always brings you face-to-face with the purposes, priorities and goals of the Almighty. It exposes you to His will. Our Lord's core values are always folded into His Word, forming His nonnegotiable message to mankind. This message, when prayed through, leads you away from self-centered and superficial praying by directing you into the central purposes of our perfect God." (p.80) Over the years I have created a list of Scriptures to pray for myself, but rarely slowed down long enough to meditate on the connection between what I prayed and the events God allowed in my life.

I am reminded of my first meeting with the president of the ministry, one during which He asked for a brief version of my life story. Since he endorses home schooling for many reasons, including the way learning at home can spare young people from negative influences often found in public schools and universities, He jokingly commented, "For one who's been through all that (public school and college), you don't seem to have turned out too bad!" I chuckled along with him, but the comment prompted reflection, and I realized that a number of Christian friends had fallen prey to temptations in high school and college that I somehow avoided. "What made me different?" I wondered.

While praying later on that week, the Holy Spirit reminded me of something I habitually prayed since the age of 14 or so. At that time, I was challenged by a speaker at a conference to ask God to cover me with His armor on a daily basis, after the manner described in Ephesians 6. As I reflected that day, I realized that God had answered my prayer. The armor formed an invisible shield about me throughout those years and though surrounded by temptations, like a child picking daisies at the edge of a cliff, I never realized the danger or fell far into the traps that ensnared my friends and acquaintances. I know there were times I routinely prayed on the armor in the morning, only to chase after the ungodly throughout the day. Yet, God honored my prayer, and I never could catch up to those retreating from their godly heritage rather than building on it.

Because praying this portion of Scripture has so greatly impacted my life, I want to take the time here to look carefully at these verses and their application to the daily life of a Christian. After examining the armor, we will look at several other Scriptural prayers that contain vital requests for spiritual growth. Praying these regularly has changed the course of my life because I have learned to ask for spiritually significant things with eternal potential. These passages get at the heart of God's will for my life and take me beyond the trite prayers formed by my limited intellect.

Burr explains this sentiment thusly, "Through Scripture praying, we not only use His Word to properly format our prayers, but this same Word is used by God to nourish, encourage and instruct our souls. The Word of God is living and active; it pierces and quickens one's heart; it exposes and judges our thoughts and motives; it lays bare our hearts in preparation for becoming pure; it prepares us to become recipients of His mercy and grace (Hebrews 4:12 – 16). It is absolute truth, and by using it properly we will not ask amiss." (p.82)

Praying Scripture has taught me to ask God to make me the person He wants me to be, rather than spending time giving God a laundry list of requests for temporal things. I hope my testimony here motivates you to learn to pray Scripture. These passages are certainly within the boundaries of God's will for your life, and I know great blessings are in store as you incorporate them into prayers for yourself and others.

EPHESIANS 6 – THE ARMOR OF GOD

"Therefore take up the whole armor of God, that you may be able to withstand in the evil day, and having done all, to stand firm. Stand therefore, having fastened on the belt of truth, and having put on the breastplate of righteousness, and, as shoes for your feet, having put on the readiness given by the gospel of peace. In all circumstances take up the shield of faith, with which you can extinguish all the flaming darts of the evil one; and take the helmet of salvation, and the sword of the Spirit, which is the word of God, praying at all times in the Spirit, with all prayer and supplication." (Ephesians 6:13 – 18a)

The first piece of armor God commands us to "put on" is the belt of truth. Truth is the most important place to begin each day. Jesus says in John 14:6, "I am the way, and the truth, and the life. No one comes to the Father except through me." We do well to remember our need of Christ, the ultimate, unchanging truth, first thing each morning. Meditating on truth also serves to remind us of the following:

- our identity in Christ – precious royalty belonging to the King of Kings,
- our purpose in life – to glorify God as we delight in Him,
- our goal for living – to point others to Christ,
- our source of power and victory – the grace God makes available for us to fulfill His call on our lives as we do the work we're called to do.

The breastplate of righteousness is the second piece of armor God commands us to appropriate. The breastplate guards the heart and the vital organs. In a spiritual sense, we ask God to cover our soul: the mind, will and emotions, with His righteousness when we put on this piece of armor. Our daily desire should be to walk in righteousness and point others to the righteousness of Christ. Daniel 12:3 says, "And those who are wise shall shine like the brightness of the sky above; and those who turn many to righteousness, like the stars forever and ever."

I cannot think about the next piece of armor without remembering the words of Isaiah 52:7, "How beautiful upon the mountains are the feet of him who brings good news, who publishes peace, who brings good news of happiness, who publishes salvation, who says to Zion, 'Your God reigns'." The shoes of peace hopefully guide us into peace-making each day, whether that involves telling someone the good news of Christ's saving grace and helping them make peace with their Creator, or bringing peace to brothers and sisters in Christ who cross our paths on a given day. In a world full of turmoil, peace is one of the greatest gifts we possess, and our enjoyment of it multiplies as we pass it on to others.

The shield of faith is the fourth piece of armor, one that we move around in order to block the darts of the enemy as He attempts to steal our joy and kill our witness. Hebrews

11:6 comes to mind as I pray on this piece of armor, "And without faith it is impossible to please him, for whoever would draw near to God must believe that he exists and that he rewards those who seek him." Faith begins with acknowledging Christ as Savior and Lord and trusting the truth of the promises of Scripture. Another verse I often think of when considering issues of faith is the cry of the man who said, "I believe; help my unbelief." (Mark 9:24) As much as I desire and pray for strong faith, I often find myself lacking. Rather than being embarrassed by my need, routinely praying on the armor gives me an opportunity to beseech God to increase the faith He already knows I lack.

Psalm 27:1 says, "The Lord is my light and my salvation; whom shall I fear? The Lord is the strength of my life; of whom shall I be afraid?" (KJV) This verse corresponds with the fifth piece of armor: the helmet of salvation. Since the helmet goes on the head, I use this piece to remind me to ask the Lord to guard my thoughts as well as my words each day. I need Him to keep my thoughts from wandering down ungodly paths, and I need His help to keep from speaking aloud every thought that runs through my mind. The roots of this request lie in Psalm 19:14, "Let the words of my mouth, and the meditation of my heart, be acceptable in thy sight, O LORD, my strength, and my redeemer." (KJV)

The last two pieces of armor are the Sword of the Spirit – God's Word –and the power of prayer. Hebrews 4:12 says, "For the word of God is living and active, sharper than any two-edged sword, piercing to the division of soul and of spirit, of joints and of marrow, and discerning the thoughts and intentions of the heart." This is an offensive weapon, given to us to discern among the philosophies, paradigms, propaganda, and personalities that surround us each day. It goes hand in hand with the discipline of prayer: our access to the only One who knows all the answers and goes before us in every way.

God has given us enormous resources and protection in the armor He provides, yet prior to hearing this speaker, I failed to see the relevance of employing it on a daily basis. When we, as believers, with the endless reservoir of God's power at our beck and call, choose to ignore it and face each day unarmed, encountering difficulties, challenges, and tragedies should not surprise us.

Consider the folly of a soldier who rises at dawn one morning and decides to leave his tent for a quick stroll around the camp's perimeter in his pajamas. As he stands outside the relative safety of his tent and stretches, he looks around but does not see anything threatening, so he meanders away carelessly. Would we be surprised if he walked right into an ambush and was captured? The battles we face each day are no less significant than the soldier's, and those are just the ones we see. The more intense fighting occurs in the spiritual realm.

In his preamble to the armor passage, Paul urges the believers in Ephesus to put on the whole armor in preparation for facing the enemy. He reminds them, "We do not wrestle against flesh and blood, but against the rulers, against the authorities, against the cosmic powers over this present darkness, against the spiritual forces of evil in the heavenly places." (6:12) This is the real reason for putting on the armor each day: preparing for battle. God alone knows what awaits us beyond the secure perimeter of our bedroom. It is foolish to not take the time to "dress for the day" spiritually, just as we do physically.

Not only is this a vital passage to pray in the morning, I find I return to it whenever I find myself in a situation where I feel threatened. The night of September 11, 2001, after watching hours of footage reliving the horrors of the terrorist attacks on New York City and Washington, D.C., fear was almost a tangible presence in my room. Every time I closed my eyes, I saw an airplane slamming into the second tower of the World Trade Center, flames exploding, people falling, and buildings crumbling. As I tried to breathe deeply and go to sleep, I began to pray through the list of armor, piece by piece, quoting as many other related verses as I could remember. Slowly, the peace of God displaced the horror and fear and brought comfort. Such is the power of prayer, and the power of claiming these verses for my own.

DEVELOPING ATTITUDES THAT INFLUENCE OTHERS

While attending a "Basic Youth Conflicts" seminar as a teenager, Bill Gothard, the teacher, challenged us to ask God to develop specific attitudes in our lives in order to effectively influence others in godliness. I soon added this to my daily prayer list, asking God to build a spirit of reverence, gratefulness, service, and meekness into my life. This prayer, in addition to praying on the armor, has become a staple in my daily diet of prayer. Let me briefly explain the significance of each of these attitudes.

One definition of reverence is a humble awareness of how a sovereign God is at work through the people and events in my life to produce the character of Christ in me. I have clung to this through the months of recovering my health, for I realize that God is using these circumstances to make me more like His Son. I have had a relatively easy life, rarely needing to trust God for basics such as food, clothing, and shelter. Losing my health for a time forced me to recognize my need for breath to sustain life, strength to swing my legs out of bed, mental acuity to think clearly and emotional stamina for interacting with people. Recognizing my needs kindled humility and sparked new dimensions of gratefulness. One of the most significant was realizing that suffering expanded my capacity to care for others experiencing pain. Gratefulness increased as I saw God use my testimony of weakness to strengthen and encourage others experiencing hard things.

Developing a grateful spirit means learning to appreciate the ways in which the investments of God and others benefit my life. During my high school years, my mother started a family tradition of having us each write in a "gratefulness journal" at Thanksgiving and then share our thoughts around the bountiful table. This practice began to instill in me the realization that I am a composite of the investments of many people: my parents, my siblings, friends, school teachers, church leaders, college professors, seminar leaders, authors, relatives, and acquaintances. Each has invested something of their life into mine and helped make me the person I am today.

God, of course, rightly deserves the most credit for who I am. Without His permission, I never would have been born. I had no choice of nationality, ethnicity, gender, social status, parents, siblings, appearance, intellectual ability or time in history. I am incredibly blessed, and gratefulness grows each time I stop to count the blessings that define my life's boundaries.

The attitude of serving grows as I learn more of Christ, for He was the greatest example of a servant to ever walk the earth. If I intend to follow His example, I must humble myself and attend to the needs of others. If I refuse, I will never acquire an inkling of an idea of what it meant for Him to set aside the splendors of heaven and humble Himself to become a man. He taught the disciples in Mark 10:44, "Whoever would be first among you must be slave (bondservant) of all."

Jesus backed up statements like this with His example in John 13 when He washed the disciples' feet. Jesus "rose from supper. He laid aside his outer garments, and taking a towel, tied it around his waist." (John 13:4) He took four key steps that anyone aspiring to servanthood should emulate. First, He rose from the table. He took the initiative and got up from his comfortable place to minister to the needs of others. Secondly, he laid aside his garments, that which would hinder him from completing the task at hand. Next he picked up a towel; he assembled the necessary tools for serving. Finally, he tied it around his own waist. He did not wait for someone to recognize his intent and volunteer help or praise. He quietly prepared himself and then he washed the dirty feet of the men about to abandon him in his greatest hour of need. What an example!

I saw a living illustration of this spirit of service while traveling with a choral group the summer between my sophomore and junior years in college. Each night after our concert, we were divided among the members of the host church who kept us in their homes overnight. While in Budapest, Hungary, I spent one night with a young college student named Nora.

Nora's home life had not been easy and it was with a measure of relief that she was able to scrape enough rent together each month to live by herself in a tiny apartment. It wasn't much, but she graciously shared her space with me that particular night. While preparing for bed, I noticed what I thought was a washing machine tucked into the cramped space in her bathroom. Since doing laundry was a luxury, I asked if it would be possible to clean a few things while I was with her. In her broken English, she indicated that if I would give her my clothes, she would be happy to wash them for me. Thinking that would require little more than tossing them in the machine, I gladly handed them over.

A little while later I knocked on the bathroom door to say goodnight. Nora opened the door with a sheepish look and I was stunned to see my clothes soaking in the sink. To this day I don't know what kind of contraption I thought I saw in the bathroom, but she was carefully washing my clothes by hand. Her humble act of service surprised me because it went so far beyond what I considered normal bounds of hospitality. Ever since, when I think of a true servant, I think of Nora and the way she demonstrated the spirit of Christ to me by meeting such a practical need for me that night.

The final attitude of influence is meekness. This character quality grows as I learn to accept that my Sovereign God is working through both the pleasant, and the painful, circumstances of my life. These He permits and employs in order to correct me and purify my character. Only through acceptance can I experience true and lasting peace. Embracing as God's will both the good and the bad demonstrates faith and a confidence that God is still on the throne, even when I am hurting. He watches my pain, perhaps from the same place He witnessed the agony of His own Son. I *can* trust Him, and if I desire peace this side of eternity, I *must* trust Him. I love Babbie Mason's insightful song, "Trust His Heart:"

> God is too wise to be mistaken.
> God is too good to be unkind.
> So when you don't understand;
> when you can't see His plan;
> when you can't trace His hand,
> trust His heart.

As God develops these characteristics in my life in accordance with His will and in answer to my prayer, my capacity for trust and love deepens, and hopefully my countenance reflects a growing peace.

PAUL'S POWER PRAYERS

Through learning to pray on the armor and ask God to build attitudes of influence in my life, the Lord whetted my appetite for praying according to Scripture and its principles. In more recent years, Paul's prayers in Colossians 1 and Ephesians 1 and 3 have challenged me. I began praying them for students in Advanced EXCEL, but then continued beseeching the Lord to fulfill in my life the things I requested for these students. I realized that I would never construct prayers containing such grand requests, so I stuck with these and believe I am seeing some of the results, even through the years of illness I have experienced.

Paul writes in Colossians, "And so, from the day we heard, we have not ceased to pray for you, asking that you may be filled with the knowledge of his will in all spiritual wisdom and understanding, so as to walk in a manner worthy of the Lord, fully pleasing to him, bearing fruit in every good work and increasing in the knowledge of God. May you be strengthened with all power, according to his glorious might, for all endurance and patience with joy, giving thanks to the Father, who has qualified you to share in the inheritance of the saints in light. He has delivered us from the domain of darkness and transferred us to the kingdom of his beloved Son, in whom we have redemption, the forgiveness of sins." (1:9-14).

Let's look more closely at what Paul is requesting in this prayer. He asks first that God fill each of the believers with the knowledge of His will so that they grow in wisdom and understanding of spiritual matters. Then He prays that all they do would be worthy of the Heavenly Father, bear fruit for His kingdom, and further conform them to His image. He desires for them to grow in strength, patience, longsuffering, and joyfulness. Finally, he thanks God for the privileges of being part of the Body of Christ, an heir to the eternal inheritance of the sons and daughters of the King of Kings. The last verse reminds them of who they are: redeemed ones, grafted into a new kingdom with access to unimaginable power. Each of these vital truths becomes more real to me as I meditate on them during my prayer time.

In Ephesians Paul prays, "For this reason, because I have heard of your faith in the Lord Jesus and your love toward all the saints, I do not cease to give thanks for you, remembering you in my prayers, that the God of our Lord Jesus Christ, the Father of glory, may give you a spirit of wisdom and of revelation in the knowledge of him, having the eyes of your hearts enlightened, that you may know what is the hope to which he has called you, what are the riches of his glorious inheritance in the saints, and what is the immeasurable greatness of his power toward us who believe, according to the working of his great might" (1:15-19).

In this passage, Paul asks God again to increase the wisdom of the believers and their knowledge of God. He beseeches God to open the eyes of their understanding so that they realize the incredible hope and glory that exists for those called to new life in Christ. He closes with a reminder of the greatness of the power of God at work in their lives.

Ephesians 3 contains Paul's final direct prayer for this group of believers: "For this reason I bow my knees before the Father, from whom every family in heaven and on earth is named, that according to the riches of his glory he may grant you to be strengthened with power through his Spirit in your inner being, so that Christ may dwell in your hearts through faith—that you, being rooted and grounded in love, may have strength to comprehend with all the saints what is the breadth and length and height and depth, and to know the love of Christ that surpasses knowledge, that you may be filled with all the fullness of God.(3:14-19)

Paul asks for the Ephesians, and I ask God to answer these specific requests for myself. First of all, I want God to strengthen my mind, will, and emotions through the indwelling power of the Holy Spirit so that I can face wisely the elements of ungodliness in our postmodern culture. I want an abiding faith in Christ, one that clings to Him in trust even when I hurt. I desire to understand the love of God for me so that my trust in Him is unshakeable, and I never yield to the temptation to question whether or not He really has my best interests at heart. I also want to know more of the love of Christ, the kind of love that willingly poured itself out to provide salvation for His people.

The next request in this prayer is to be filled with all the fullness of God; this is the opposite of self-centeredness. In verse 20, Paul acknowledges that God is able to accomplish "exceeding abundantly above all that we ask or think," (KJV) and I usually end my prayer by asking Him to really do that in my life and in the lives of those I love. This is so much more satisfying than quickly running through a list of names saying, "God, please bless Mom, Dad, Amy, Adam, Julianne, etc." This passage has greatly expanded the boundaries of my prayer life and multiplied the blessings I receive as God responds to my bolder and broader requests.

Learning to pray Scripture has deepened my trust in God, further developed my understanding of His Word and increased my boldness in praying for others. It has expanded my understanding of His call on my life as well because I spend the bulk of my time asking Him to develop who I *am*, not what I *do*. Now that I have a list of all the special verses God has given to point me in the direction of His specific call on my life, I can also pray through these for motivation and guidance. As I meditate on them, my awe for God and His purposes increases. My spiritual needs and eternal purpose become a higher priority than my temporal wants, and I walk in obedience to Christ's command, "But seek first the kingdom of God, and his righteousness; and all these things will be added unto you." (Matthew 6:33)

CHAPTER SEVEN

The Beauty of Discipleship: A Laser versus a Floodlight

*"It is an inspiring thought that one small pebble
dropped in the sea of history
can produce waves of grace that break on distant shores
hundreds of years later and thousands of miles away."*
John Piper

One day a group of religious and community leaders
came to Jesus to question Him. One of them asked Him
to name the greatest commandment in the Law of Moses in
an attempt to trick Him into indicting Himself. Jesus' answer
effectively silenced His examiners and has set the boundaries
for true believers ever since. "And he said to him, 'You shall
love the Lord your God with all your heart and with all your
soul and with all your mind. This is the great and first commandment. And a second is like it: You shall love your
neighbor as yourself. On these two commandments depend
all the Law and the Prophets'." (Matthew 22:37-40)

Jesus is the only man to ever fulfill this law completely.

The ways in which He used His time reflected His understanding of the Law of God and set a sterling example for us to follow. He demonstrated His love for God by making time with Him the highest priority of His life, spending precious hours alone with the Father in prayer. In this way the will of the Father consumed His entire being: heart, soul, and mind. Jesus ultimately demonstrated perfect love for His "neighbors" by dying on the cross and rising victoriously after defeating the powers of death and hell. But prior to His death, He showed His love for others in countless ways, among them healing the sick, teaching the multitudes, and blessing the children.

The way Jesus nurtured the disciples further illustrated love for them. His investment in this motley group changed their lives for eternity, and their consequent investment in thousands sent ripples of everlasting change around the world. It is interesting that Jesus left work for the disciples to do after He returned to heaven to intercede and rule at the right hand of the Father. We might have expected Him to complete all the work Himself. His willingness to leave some things undone and to entrust the disciples with the responsibility to carry on the work indicate His confidence in them and in the Father's master plan. We can learn a great deal about His approach to ministry by studying the way He trained the disciples and then gave them a significant role in multiplying the message of His life.

I find it fascinating – and freeing – to realize that Jesus did not try to do everything Himself. He prepared for His life calling through study in the synagogue as a growing man, by baptism at the hand of His cousin John, and spending 40 days alone in the wilderness in prayer and fasting. But once He was ready to pursue His calling full time, He immediately began recruiting disciples, training them, and giving them opportunities to work, both alongside Him and on their own. In Mark 1:16-20 we see Him call Simon, Andrew, James and

John. The next day He invites Philip and Nathanael to join the group. His company of followers continued to grow, and not long after calling these specifically, He identified a total of twelve, forming an inner circle of disciples. Mark records His purposes for choosing these. "And he appointed twelve (whom he also named apostles) so that they might be with him and he might send them out to preach and have authority to cast out demons." (Mark 3:14-15)

Jesus did not surround Himself with people just for the pleasure of their company, though that was certainly one purpose. His vision for them was much greater. He taught them how to minister healing to the body by tapping into God's power through prayer. He gave them the ability to cast out demons and thus free the mind, will, and emotions of those in torment. He also showed them how to heal the soul: through preaching the good news of the gospel. As they spent time with Him, He prepared the disciples to carry on His work, and He gave them opportunities to practice while He was still there in the flesh to provide counsel, feedback, and additional training. He defined the boundaries and invited them to enjoy the blessing of God as they walked with Him.

Shortly after singling out the twelve, He began sending them out to teach and heal. In Luke 10:1, He commissions a larger group of seventy to go out by twos with the same assignment as the twelve. Why did He do this? Christ had the greatest mission of anyone to ever walk the earth, and yet He did not insist on doing it all Himself. He knew the Father's plan involved continuing the work of redemption through the medium of the church, and this required trained men to preach the gospel, nurture converts, and care for the needs of the church body. By allowing these men to "get their feet wet" while Jesus still lived on earth, He included them in His work and gave them valuable training for the future.

Just as the testing in the wilderness refined Him and

prepared Him for His mission, Jesus knew these times of going out and coming in served to refine and prepare those who would carry on His work. Their struggles and victories during these initial ventures paved the way for both the obstacles and opportunities down the road. Discipleship is a process, with each interaction and experience laying a foundation for the time when the student becomes the teacher and so begins the process from a new perspective.

During this time, Christ also demonstrated the proper way to fulfill the commission He would give the disciples before returning to heaven: "Go therefore and make disciples of all nations, baptizing them in the name of the Father and of the Son and of the Holy Spirit, teaching them to observe all that I have commanded you." (Matthew 28:18-20a) Many times, this passage is used to emphasize the importance of preaching the gospel. What we sometimes overlook here is that Christ really sent the disciples out to teach, baptize and disciple – not just evangelize.

Simply sharing the gospel and leading someone in a "sinner's prayer" does not give them the tools necessary to live a life devoted to God. Instruction requires time, and it is impossible to teach others to observe the commands of Christ without spending time with them. We need look no further than America to see the devastating results of a lack of instruction. When a majority of people claim to be Christian but sin runs rampant in their society, something is desperately wrong. Jesus invested His life in the disciples to a degree that equipped them to invest in others themselves. This type of replication marks discipleship that revolutionizes a culture and impacts the world.

How does this apply to those of us who know God has called us and who desire to obey the command to love others by serving them through a lifestyle of ministry? First, it should remind us immediately that discipleship is a command that falls within the boundaries for all Christians; it is not simply a special calling for some. Second, it should expose the folly of trying to do all the work myself rather than risk delegating to someone who will not do it "my way." If anyone had cause to do that, it was Christ. Since He refused to fall into that temptation, I should reject that approach for myself.

I have certainly had times where I put my trust in someone to complete a project and watched them fail in areas I know I could have succeeded. This happens to us all whether in the ministry, on the job, or in the home. Just ask the mother who delegates the task of doing the laundry to a child only to find a load of whites turned pink because a red shirt got put in the wrong pile. Failures among those we nurture or teach should motivate us to search our own hearts to see if we should have communicated differently or more thoroughly. But we should also see them as opportunities for learning and growth. A wise leader will turn shortcomings into illustrations of what not to do in the future and in this way give value to failures. Because Jesus called disciples to Him, allowed them to share His work and turned failures into opportunities to learn, He effectively built His vision for saving the world into them.

Christ's example provides many principles for discipleship that can spare us from burn out if we follow them. I know now that my illness resulted, at least in part, from attempting to do more than one person could possibly do. I ignored my boundaries and am paying the price. My desire to please God and accomplish great things for His kingdom drove me to exhaustion, because I did not follow Christ's example and learn to effectively share the load. How did Jesus, as a leader with an enormous mission, work with others and escape the burn out running rampant in the church today?

PRINCIPLE 1 – REALIZE THE BOUNDARIES OF DISCIPLESHIP

The first and most important key is the one already mentioned: discipleship. Knowing His own time was limited, Jesus purposely invested in others who would carry on once He returned to heaven. While Jesus Himself focused His ministry on a small group: the Jews, He charged His followers with taking His message to the world. Each of them would be called to a specific group so that the gospel spread, "in Jerusalem, and in all Judea and Samaria, and to the end of the earth" (Acts 1:8b).

Although He carried a burden for all the peoples of the world, Jesus' deepest ministry focused on an even smaller group than the Jews: the disciples. "He did not speak to them without a parable, but privately to his own disciples he explained everything." (Mark 4:34) He ensured that the disciples understood more than the multitudes even though teaching them required extra time and energy. Even among the twelve, three spent more time with Him than the rest. "And after six days Jesus took with him Peter and James, and John his brother, and led them up a high mountain by themselves." (Matthew 17:1). Then another time, "Jesus went with them to a place called Gethsemane, and he said to his disciples, 'Sit here, while I go over there and pray.' And taking with him Peter and the two sons of Zebedee, he began to be sorrowful and troubled." (Matthew 26:36-37a)

By establishing a narrow but deep focus, Jesus replicated His life with the force of a laser beam, rather than stretching beyond His limits like a floodlight that illuminates but has little energy to effect change. The group of disciples was small, but Christ trained them so effectively that they turned their world upside down in just a few short years after He returned to heaven and sent the Holy Spirit to comfort, empower, and guide them. Too often, we spread ourselves so thin that our impact is a mile wide and an inch deep. Jesus did not do this.

His ministry expanded through the lives of His followers. He poured Himself into them, and then His ministry multiplied as they poured themselves into others.

As the chaplain of the student government during my senior year at Messiah, I was "called" to minister to the student body of over 2,000. I invested in them through prayer and an occasional devotional in chapel, but a deeper ministry focused on a smaller group: leaders of Bible studies in the dormitories. I met regularly with this group of 30 – 40 student leaders and encouraged them in their individual ministries. But even this group did not receive my most focused energies. I reserved that for a group of four: the chaplains of each class. With this group I prayed and shared my hopes for the school and endeavored to pass on a heart of devotion to Christ.

This scenario repeated itself during my years in Dallas. I initially came to invest in the lives of the EXCEL students: groups of 80 – 100 who lived here for eight weeks at a time. After a couple years, we started the Advanced EXCEL ministry, and I focused my energies on smaller classes of eight to twelve who participated in intense discipleship for five months and learned to disciple others by developing groups of their own at home. Though I gave a part of my heart to each of the 100 plus young ladies who participated in Advanced EXCEL over the six years I served as the director, my deepest sharing occurred with those who assisted me in leading the program. These young ladies served alongside me one at a time and I sought to transfer the passion of my heart of hearts: to share the love of Christ and replicate His life in the lives of other young women.

In both situations, in college and in Dallas, I have seen the wisdom of Jesus' approach. The more intimate the relationship and the deeper the investment of time and shared growth in the ways of Christ, the greater the impact on the lives of others. By passing on a passion for Christ, God's ministry through me increases via the lives of those I disciple. In this way, my personal boundaries may appear small, but they expand through the hands of those in whom I invest. And, we all receive the blessing of serving the Lord and encouraging others.

During the first few months of recovery when I spent much of my time in bed, I struggled with feelings of helplessness, even worthlessness, because my ability to minister was hindered. One afternoon the Lord prompted me to consider the ministry now in motion through those I have discipled. I pondered the way He led some to mission work overseas, some to teach and disciple children, others to serve government leaders and still more to serve their families at home. I realized then that, in His grace, God is using me to reach the world, but right now He is using those in whom I have invested more than the work of my own hands. I found meditating on this principle enormously freeing: if the Son of God worked with and through others to realize His God-given vision for the world, then certainly I can trust God to work in the same way through the life and ministry He's given me. I remain faithful by remaining focused, not by trying to single-handedly meet the needs of the world.

We see the effects of a focused vision in the lives of others in Scripture. John the Baptist concentrated His energies on a relatively small group, the Jews, and He had one simple message: Repent. "John appeared, baptizing in the wilderness and proclaiming a baptism of repentance for the forgiveness of sins." (Mark 1:4) He knew His job also included preparing the way for the Messiah and He boldly proclaimed, "Repent, for the kingdom of God is at hand." (Matthew 3:2) He stayed focused and kept the message simple rather than leaving the straightforward approach and branching off into new areas. Later in the history of the church, we see Peter focus His energies on winning the Jews to Christ. Paul, in turn, takes His message primarily to the Gentiles. Though He travels extensively, He stays tuned in to the Holy Spirit and remains within the limits of the Spirit's leading. "And they went through the region of Phrygia and Galatia, *having been forbidden by the Holy Spirit to speak the word in Asia.* And when they had come up to Mysia, they attempted to go into Bithynia, *but the Spirit of Jesus did not allow them.*" (Acts 16:6-7, emphasis mine)

PRINCIPLE 2 – SET EMOTIONAL BOUNDARIES

A second key to preventing burn out that I see in reading through the gospels is that Jesus limited the number of intimate relationships in His life. Though He ministered to many (see Matthew nine for examples), He carefully chose those He allowed into the inner circle and invested differently in these select few. We see the contrast in Luke 6. In verses 12-16, He chooses the twelve after a night of prayer. He sought His Father's direction for whom to allow close and He interacted differently with these than with the multitudes who came to hear Him preach (verses 17-19). Though verse 19 says, "and all the crowd sought to touch him" at the end of the day, when the teaching was over, only a few left with the main speaker.

Setting boundaries for accessibility and intimacy can be a difficult thing for a person with a public life. I have certainly found this true for me, and what I do is small compared to women who speak around the country or on the radio, wives whose husbands pastor large churches, or those serving in government office. Still, because the Lord has given me opportunities to work with many young ladies over the years, many want my time and attention. Girls feel close to me because they heard me speak at a conference or spent time with us in Dallas. If I tried to give each of them an equal amount of time and energy, I would wear out. I find it immensely comforting to learn from the life of Jesus that He does not call me to invest equally in every person who crosses my path. He expects me to disciple, yes, but not to constantly socialize.

PRINCIPLE 3 – ACCEPT REALISTIC EXPECTATIONS OF OTHERS

A third principle I observe in the way Jesus interacted with the disciples is that He had realistic expectations. Jesus knew that even His closest friends would let Him down ... they desert Him in the garden (Mark 14:50), Peter denies him during His trial (John 18), and Judas betrays Him. John records this sad statement in chapter 6 verses 70-71, "Did I not choose you, the Twelve? And yet one of you is a devil. He spoke of Judas the son of Simon Iscariot, for he, one of the Twelve, was going to betray him." Because Jesus accepted the reality that they would not do everything the way He would, that they would fail, He was able to continue investing in them.

If Christ experienced disappointment with those in whom He invested, we can be confident we will too. Even when we choose friends and disciples carefully, some may fall away or disappoint us with the choices they make. We must not allow that to embitter us or deter us from the call to disciple others. Though His followers gave Him cause for grief, because Jesus did not give up on them, all but Judas proved their commitment to Him in the end.

This principle particularly challenged me when a former student whose friendship I cherished had an affair with a married man. The two ran away together and he divorced his wife in order to marry this young woman that carried his child. The news pierced my heart like a knife. After all that I (and many others) had invested in this young lady, she chose to reject the truth and actively pursue a life of sin. After a time, the couple publicly repented of their sinful choices, but it has been hard to forgive and want to invest in her life again.

God has used this situation to help me identify with the

feelings of betrayal and rejection Christ experienced. He has also used it to shine a spotlight on the shortcomings and failures in my life that disappoint Him. If I desire His grace and mercy in the face of my sin, then I must be willing to forgive any and all who I feel reject me or betray my confidence. Coming to grips with the sin in my heart should enable me to release others from my expectations and love them through failures just as Christ did. It should also give me the grace to obey Galatians 6:1, "Brothers, if anyone is caught in any transgression, you who are spiritual should restore him in a spirit of gentleness. Keep watch on yourself, lest you too be tempted."

Scripture is full of examples of those who God used in mighty ways even after incredible shortcomings. I recently read Francine Rivers' novella about the life of Bathsheba and was reminded that this adulterous woman bore the future king of Israel, and God chose to engraft her into the lineage of His own Son after she repented of her sin. If we intend to live a life of ministry to people, we must be willing to work with them through failures and visualize God's greater purposes for their lives. In so doing, we pass on the kind of mercy Christ showed when he restored men like Peter, and perhaps encourage the next generation of world-changers.

PRINCIPLE 4 – LIMIT THE DETOURS FROM YOUR CALLING

The fourth principle in Jesus' approach to ministry is personally very freeing because of my tendency to want to do more than I possibly have time or energy for. An acute awareness of His calling in life motivated Jesus and He kept any detours to that calling limited and brief, the exception rather than the rule.

Christ identified the boundaries of His calling and focused His energies there rather than falling prey to the temptation of trying to meet all the needs all the time. In Mark 7:24-30 He actually rejects the pleas of a woman for help because she was Greek. His words to her seem harsh in verse 27, "And he said to her, 'Let the children be fed first, for it is not right to take the children's bread and throw it to the dogs'." His meaning was clear: He was called to a particular group and she was not part of it. However, because she persisted, He relented and granted her request and healed her daughter. This scene did not prompt Him to expand His ministry to the Greeks at that time, but He did expend energy briefly in this particular situation.

Luke 7:1-10 provides another illustration. A Roman centurion begged Him to heal a dying servant, and Jesus responded to His request. Though He did not change His approach and begin preaching to the Roman community in the region, He used the opportunity to heal this one to highlight the centurion's faith and challenge the Jews who lacked it.

Another time, Jesus stunned His disciples by taking a detour through Samaria and talking with an adulterous woman. Her conversion sparked the fires of revival in her town, and Jesus devoted two days to preaching and teaching the gospel there. Nonetheless, He only spared two days, and this did not prompt a change in His overall strategy to focus His attention on His own Jewish people.

Jesus knew a divided vision would not prosper. With the limitations of humanity, no one person can reach every other person in the world with the gospel or disciple every new believer in every part of the world. This is why knowing and understanding one's calling is so important. If everyone does their part, we will live to realize the fulfillment of the Great Commission, but one person can not possibly do it alone. Knowing how and when to limit the detours and remain within our boundaries is difficult and requires much prayer.

Several years ago I read an insightful book by Stephen

Covey entitled, <u>Seven Habits of Highly Effective People</u>. One of the concepts he develops is the difference between one's circle of concern and circle of influence. The circle of concern is large and covers many issues. For instance, poverty, world hunger, child abuse, abortion and pornography all concern me. The circle of influence, on the other hand, fits inside the circle of concern and contains those things I can actually change. I cannot alter the reality that thousands of children starve to death in countries around the world, but I could choose to sponsor (or even adopt!) one through any number of mercy ministries. Unless I am called to devote my life to promoting the freedom to choose life, I cannot do much to halt the murder of up to 4,000 babies in America each day. However, I could open my home to one scared, pregnant teenager who knows in her heart killing her baby is not the answer, but desperately needs love and support to carry it to term and learn how to care for its needs.

I do not know if this happens to others, but I used to panic at times as the gravity of the task of reaching the world weighed on my heart and mind. My circle of concern threatened to consume me for it stretched as endlessly before me as the horizon. I would weep until exhausted thinking about those in need of a Savior, those who live each day oppressed by the ravaging power of sin. Focusing on areas of concern was like shining a floodlight on the issues. The light illuminated the problems but did nothing to change them. Learning to narrow the scope of emotional investment to my actual God-given calling allowed me to channel my energies like a laser beam. A laser brightens the issue and has the power to effect change.

Jesus cared passionately and He died to provide salvation for His children in every corner of the world. In His life, we see the importance of both perspectives. The floodlight of God's glory shone through His earthly ministry, and the laser beam of His power was demonstrated on the cross.

However, even Jesus focused His energies on a relatively small "circle of influence" for most of His life, and I believe this is an important principle for us to emulate. Though spoken in a different context, I think the wisdom of Luke 11:17 applies to this concept, "But he, knowing their thoughts, said to them, 'Every kingdom divided against itself is laid waste, and a divided household falls'."

THE PRIDE OF OVEREXTENSION

When I look back on my attempts to meet needs that fell outside the scope of my calling and boundaries, I realize pride at least partially motivated me. Overextending oneself may point to that worst of spirits that forgets that God is in control and believes instead that, "It all depends on me." In this way, the circle of concern overshadows the circle of influence. This is a recipe for disaster in ministry and a strong indication that I am focusing more on the cares of the world around me than on the God Who created it all.

For one thing, God chooses whom He will use and if He gives us a part to play in expanding the work of His kingdom, we should thank Him with humble hearts. We should pray, like King David as He thought about the resources to build the temple, "But who am I, and what is my family, that I should be able to willingly make such an offering? For all things come from You, and I have only given back what is already Yours. For I am a stranger before You, a sojourner, as was my father: my days on the earth are as a shadow, and there is none that last forever. O LORD my God, all my energies and resources for building a ministry for Your holy name come from Your hand, and they are all Your own." (I Chronicles 19:14-16, paraphrase mine)

Secondly, God hates pride and will not bless the work of our hands if pride motivates it. "For everyone who exalts Himself will be humbled; but the one who humbles himself will be exalted." (Luke 18:14) He "raises up one and puts down another," and we can do nothing of lasting value without Him.

OVEREXTENDING TO MEET EXPECTATIONS

Working outside the realm of our calling may also indicate a heart influenced by the spoken or unspoken expectations of others. It is very easy to begin feeling controlled by what we believe others expect us to do, say, wear, listen to or view. This pressure can come from those I am serving, both my authorities and those to whom I actually minister.

Although it is important to show deference and obey those in authority, we must not allow unrealistic expectations to push us beyond the boundaries of what God calls us to do and be. We are called to *all* but *only* God's will for our lives, regardless of what others say or think. Just because we have the skill or ability to meet a need does not necessarily mean God is calling us to meet it. Peter understood this principle and summarized it well when he wrote, "Whoever speaks, as one who speaks oracles of God; whoever serves, as one who serves by the strength that God supplies—in order that in everything God may be glorified through Jesus Christ. To him belong glory and dominion forever and ever." (I Peter 4:11) God may be more glorified when I defer and allow someone else to have the opportunity of rising to the occasion.

THE BEAUTY OF DISCIPLESHIP

In these four principles we see the beautiful boundaries of discipleship. God does not call us to do all things by ourselves. Rather, He commissions us to disciple others in the ways of Christ and train those who share our calling to be full partners with us in a lifestyle of ministry. Christ's example challenges us to choose our intimate friends and disciples carefully while freeing us from the expectation of trying to be all things to all people and thereby overextending ourselves emotionally. His merciful acceptance and love for those who failed Him reminds us to hold our expectations of others loosely and perhaps to envision the greatest victories for those who fail the most. And finally, Jesus' impact through the ages illuminates the value of a narrow but deep focus rather than spreading one's energy among too many causes to count.

These concepts motivate me to disciple others, for I understand the command of the Great Commission and my responsibility to respond in obedience to it. In order to inspire His disciples with the confidence and hope of continuing the work He began, Jesus had to be a leader. In the next chapter, we will explore ways in which He set the standard for every leader who desires to follow His example.

CHAPTER EIGHT

Following the Leader

*"But you will receive power
when the Holy Spirit has come upon you,
and you will be my witnesses in Jerusalem
and in all Judea and Samaria and to the end of the earth."
Acts 1:8*

*P*erhaps I was always meant to be a leader. After all, I was born before my sisters and brother. At an early age I was known to organize church services in our front yard for my playmates in the neighborhood – complete with offering time. And then there was the time I told the rest of the students and parents planning for a fourth grade event that I really did not need the committee's help; I was sure I could organize everything myself. It's a wonder I survived my childhood!

My misconceptions about leadership only increased with age. Somewhere along the way I began to believe leadership roles required perfection and so appearances must be maintained at all cost. I felt I had to know all the answers and add comments to every discussion in order to fulfill the expectations I assumed others had. Whether I had to forego sleep, fun or food to keep up the façade, it was worth it as long as no one saw behind the mask. These unhealthy attitudes and actions endeared me to no one and set a standard for myself that destined me to fail sooner or later.

Since I was unwilling to do it for years, illness finally pulled back the veneer of perfection. From my sickbed the Lord reminded me that perfection this side of the grave is an unattainable goal, as futile as deciding to transform myself into an angel by determination and hard work. Perfection is an unhealthy standard because of how it drives a leader, but stubbornly adhering to it also damages those attempting to follow because it gives them a false picture of reality. They follow an example of something that is not real and thus aspire to the impossible themselves. I am learning that it is better to be authentic than perfect. This lesson has proved invaluable as I seek to lead and disciple others in the ways of Christ.

Jesus is the only perfect leader to ever walk the planet. A leader is one who "shows the way by going along with or in front of." In this chapter we will look at eleven principles He employed. Perhaps, like me, you feel you were born to lead but need help in knowing how to do that with integrity and authenticity. Or, the idea of leadership may scare you speechless. As part of the Great Commission, Jesus promised to send the Holy Spirit to give both types of His people power to share His love at home and around the world. Sharing His love is the essence of "showing the way" to those around us. Therefore, each of us is called to lead within the boundaries of God's plan for our lives. By embracing the power He provides through the Holy Spirit, each one of us can incorporate these elements of leadership into our lives and experience the blessing of "going along with or in front of" those in our homes, churches, communities and workplaces.

HE CHOSE HIS ANSWERS CAREFULLY

Jesus did not feel obligated to answer every question. For example, in Mathew 16:1-4, the Pharisees and Sadducees approach Him asking for a sign from heaven. Jesus discerned their intent to tempt Him, and He refused to give them a specific answer. He understood enough about their character to realize that no answer would satisfy this group. These men jealously desired His downfall, and He refused to play into their wicked plot. The decision to answer carefully showed great wisdom and understanding of human nature.

Matthew 21:23-27 provides another example of Jesus' ability to discern the intent of His examiners and answer wisely. In this passage, the chief priests and elders question Jesus' authority. He responds with a question for them, "I also will ask you one question, and if you tell me the answer, then I also will tell you by what authority I do these things. The baptism of John, from where did it come? From heaven or from man?" These men refuse to answer because they realize they are in a no-win situation. Siding with either position will incur the angst of those who hold to the other, so they hold their tongues. So, Jesus likewise holds His and avoids their poorly concealed trap.

While shrewd in answering – or declining to answer – His enemies, Jesus was quick to answer the honest questions of His disciples. He clarifies for them what He merely hints at to the multitudes. In Matthew 13 they ask why He speaks so often in parables and He replies, "To you it has been given to know the secrets of the kingdom of heaven, but to them it has not been given." (verse 11) Throughout the gospels we have examples of Christ giving more information to His select few, thus equipping them to carry on the work when He is gone.

The ability to wisely discern the intent behind the inquiry sets a leader apart from others who blithely answer every question posed to them. This is a critical skill for any person who desires to lead others, particularly if their leadership puts them in the public eye. Christian leaders need to learn to answer eloquently but avoid the traps set by those who disagree with them, particularly those intent on publicizing their answers. They must also learn to invest answers wisely in those destined, God willing, to become leaders themselves.

HE UNDERSTOOD AND ACCEPTED THE LONELINESS OF LEADERSHIP

Jesus accepted the fact that leadership is often lonely. He must have felt this as He interacted with His family and disciples, since they misunderstood His motives, teachings and actions at times throughout His ministry. I wonder if the loneliness was particularly poignant when He took Peter, James and John with Him to the place we now call the Mount of Transfiguration. His three closest followers accompanied Him on this short journey and He "was transfigured before them, and his face shone like the sun, and his clothes became white as light. And behold, there appeared to them Moses and Elijah, talking with him." (Matthew 17:2-3) The disciples respond with wonder and amazement, so transfixed that they ask if they should build tabernacles on the mountaintop and stay there. At that point, the cloud of God's presence covers them and He instructs them to hear the words of His beloved Son. As they descend later that day, Jesus has to explain once again that He came, not to establish an earthly kingdom or a mountaintop tabernacle, but rather to suffer for a greater cause than the disciples can imagine.

His suffering was a concept that none seemed to understand until after His death. This certainly must have felt lonely as Jesus anticipated the pain to come and realized that no one else could comprehend, much less appreciate what He was about to do. John 8:21-30 describes one such scene of misunderstanding. Jesus says, "I am going away, and you will seek me, and you will die in your sin. Where I am going, you cannot come." (verse 21). He speaks of His suffering, and they think He plans to commit suicide. They question who He is, yet again, and they refuse to believe that He is the Son of God and speaks to them about His Heavenly Father (verse 27). Jesus realized that they would only ever understand after the fact, after they witnessed His death and resurrection. "So Jesus said to them, 'When you have lifted up the Son of Man, then you will know that I am He, and that I do nothing on my own authority, but speak just as the Father taught me'." (verse 28).

He continues in verse 29, and His words should resonate deeply with every leader who has been misunderstood and maligned for following His God-given vision. "And he who sent me is with me. He has not left me alone, for I always do the things that are pleasing to him." Many misunderstood Jesus. One of his comforts was that He was doing the will of the Father and thus was not ultimately alone. Leaders must look to God to meet their deepest needs because He alone will never leave, misunderstand, or betray them. Remembering this principle comforts me when I feel alone, sometimes even among other believers.

HE MODELED HUMILITY

The best and most loved leaders are those who are humble. Jesus modeled humility and deference and highly valued it in others. In Matthew 18:3-5, Jesus admonishes the disciples, "Truly, I say to you, unless you turn and become like children, you will never enter the kingdom of heaven. Whoever humbles himself like this child is the greatest in the kingdom of heaven. Whoever receives one such child in my name receives me." Luke records an incident that highlights Jesus' ire with those who strove for positions of greatness rather than humility. When the disciples argued about their rank and title, He challenged them not to be like unbelievers who hold their positions over the heads of others. Jesus said, "Rather, let the greatest among you become as the youngest, and the leader as one who serves." (Luke 22:26)

Jesus concentrated His energies on doing "good works" rather than seeking acclaim. Mark 1:21-28 gives one example of this principle in practice. Jesus arrives in Capernaum and goes to the synagogue to teach. While there, a person with a demon shouts at Him and identifies Him as the "Holy One of God." Rather than encouraging the publicity, Jesus rebukes the demon and heals the man. Another time, some urged Jesus to reveal His true nature and broadcast His identity. Instead, Jesus resisted the temptation to assert His place and answered, "If I glorify myself, my glory is nothing. It is my Father who glorifies me, of whom you say, 'He is our God'." (John 8:54)

HE KNEW HOW TO GRACIOUSLY ACCEPT PRAISE

All of the gospel writers record Jesus' triumphal entry into Jerusalem. As the people shouted, waved palm branches and created a path for the donkey with their own clothing, Jesus entered the city for His final days of ministry. His example that day demonstrates another important principle of leadership. Though a model of humility, Jesus understood that sometimes accepting praise is appropriate, not embarrassing.

How many times have we seen people blush, stammer and look awkward as others praise them for a talented performance, insightful speech, or carefully crafted demonstration? A good leader will graciously respond to those who praise her and receive the good intentions behind the words. It is appropriate for a leader to also deflect praise by sharing how the investments of others prepared them for their position. However, she must discern the right time and place to do so. Sometimes, a pleasant smile and "thank you" are more appropriate than a long explanation of the investments leading up to the event. A gracious person knows what to say, how much to say, and when to say it as she responds to those around her.

HE COULD BE FIRM WHEN NECESSARY

Jesus was gracious on most occasions. He knew the proper etiquette for various situations and effectively interacted with those around Him whether they were sick, questioning, distressed, arrogant, or searching. He was gentle with the weak and humble, but firm with the proud and spiteful. He understood that some occasions rightly call for the display of strong emotions.

We witness one such display when Jesus enters the temple and sees the moneychangers presumably cheating the people and definitely detracting from their worship. What they were doing was wrong and a strong outburst of emotion helped effectively communicate Jesus' displeasure with their mockery of the meaning of worship. These businessmen had violated the intent of God, cheapened His worship and manipulated His regulations for a profit. Neither their traditions nor their positions intimidated Jesus. He stood up for what was right though it caused a backlash and created new enemies.

A leader must be willing to stand alone and to stand firmly for what is right even when it goes against the social, political and cultural climate. In our day we are often pressured to be "politically correct." A leader must never give in to that temptation. God's standards and priorities must be more important than risking the displeasure, condescension, and even the persecution of others. At the end of the day, I think most of us prefer to follow one who stands on his conviction rather than adjusting his views to follow the prevailing winds of public opinion.

HE REASONED DISPASSIONATELY

Jesus was able and willing to stand firm on issues that concerned Him and His Father. However, most of the time, He shared, reasoned and taught dispassionately. This channeled His energies in a positive way rather than wasting them in frustration or anger toward those who did not yet understand the truth. Anger betrays a lack of trust in God to affect change in situations and people in His own way and time. A leader must look beyond the present circumstances and focus on God's sovereignty over all times and peoples.

The ability to focus on God's sovereignty and to rest in His superintendence of the universe requires time spent meditating on His Word. The visible waves of our culture threaten to overwhelm us, just as the waves surrounded Peter when Christ invited Him to walk on the sea. As long as Peter kept His focus on his Master, he stayed above danger. As soon as he took his eyes off Jesus, he began to sink. And so do we. When we let the voices of the culture command our attention, we begin to drown in their noise, despair and helplessness. At that point, we quickly give in to waves of anger, anxiety, and frustration as we work passionately, frantically, to stem the tide of wickedness in our world. The world was no less wicked in Jesus' day. He "kept His cool" because He kept His gaze fixed on His Father. This, too, is our only hope for staying within the physical and emotional boundaries God has built into our design.

HE DISCERNED BETWEEN THE PROUD AND THE HUMBLE

Jesus had infinite patience with the humble, but no tolerance for the proud. A leader should be able to discern the character of those around him and interact with them accordingly. Jesus cared tenderly for those who recognized their need for Him. Consider the sick that sought Him for healing. He did not turn them away or treat them harshly.

When parents sought His blessing for their children, He welcomed the little, helpless ones with open arms. However, Jesus had harsh words for those who held others in contempt and thus revealed their prideful hearts. In Mark 9:42, He says, "Whoever causes one of these little ones who believe in me to sin, it would be better for him if a great millstone were hung around his neck and he were thrown into the sea." A leader must discern the appropriate approach for those He leads, giving time and attention generously to the humble and standing firmly when facing the proud.

It is easy to recognize and react to the pride we observe in others. It's humbling to realize that, unlike Christ, the sins of others that provoke the deepest reaction in me are often the very sins hiding in my own heart. A wise leader will use each confrontation with the proud to examine his own heart for the same poison and to beseech God for the antidote: humility.

HE GAVE OF HIS TIME

A leader is not a leader without followers, and people generally want to follow leaders who care for those around them. As Jesus invested time in people, they began to follow Him. Some, like the disciples, stayed with him for years. Others just briefly crossed his path. Many needed only a touch for their lives to change forever.

Mark records this scene in chapter five of his gospel. Jesus was on His way to heal the daughter of one of the prominent rulers in the synagogue, and a woman in need touched Him. "For she said, 'If I touch even his garments, I will be made well.' And immediately the flow of blood dried up, and she felt in her body that she was healed of her disease." (Mark 5:28-29) After healing this woman, Jesus continued to Jairus' home. Again, only His touch and a brief word were required. "But he ... took the child's father and mother and those who were with him and went in where the child was. Taking her by the hand he said to her, 'Talitha cumi,' which means, 'Little girl, I say to you, arise'." (Mark 5:40-41)

It is easy for a leader to think she does not have time for all the people that compete for her time and attention. It helps to remember that people are the most important part of any ministry, and caring for people is a key factor of good leadership. A good leader will always make time for a smile, a nod or a gentle touch realizing that the sovereign will of God causes her path to intersect with a particular person with a particular need at a particular point in time.

HE WAS WILLING TO SHARE THE SPOTLIGHT

Others who did good works did not threaten Jesus. He was confident in Who He was and did not need the spotlight focused on Him all the time. The disciples came to Him in Mark 9 saying, "Teacher, we saw someone casting out demons in your name, and we tried to stop him, because he was not following us. But Jesus said, 'Do not stop him, for no one who does a mighty work in my name will be able soon afterward to speak evil of me. For the one who is not against us is for us. For truly, I say to you, whoever gives you a cup of water to drink because you belong to Christ will by no means lose his reward'." (verses 38-41)

Jesus refused to spend time and energy competing for reputation or recognition. He always saw "win-win" when it came to accomplishing the Father's will, never "win-lose." A good leader recognizes that others laboring in the king-dom fields of God are responsible to Him for what they do. God calls every Christian to follow Christ's example, make disciples and extend the kingdom of Christ. How sad when some allow themselves to be deceived into squandering their energy competing with each other rather than throwing their whole heart into fulfilling their life callings.

Jesus set an excellent example by encouraging those who served God by ministering to others, rather than resenting the attention they garnered or working against them. This goes along with humility and a servant's heart. The heart of a servant-leader longs for God to get the glory and others to receive His joy. They would rather see others praised for good works than detract from those works by demanding credit for themselves. God does not call any one person to do it all anyway. This principle is a practical means of enjoying the partnerships built into the body of Christ.

HE ENVISIONED GREAT THINGS FOR HIS DISCIPLES

Along with sharing the spotlight with others, Christ visualized achievement for his followers: "Truly, truly, I say to you, whoever believes in me will also do the works that I do; and greater works than these will he do, because I am going to the Father." (John 14:12) "By this my Father is glorified, that you bear much fruit and so prove to be my disciples." (John 15:8) A good leader envisions potential for those who follow him and longs for them to achieve greater results as they build on what they learn from him.

Several years ago, I transferred leadership of the Advanced EXCEL program to two young ladies I have discipled over the years. They told me they felt overwhelmed as they faced their new levels of responsibility and told me they hoped to do "half as well" as I had done. I understood their sentiments having walked through similar situations, but I also have a great vision for them. I became their cheerleader as they became leaders for others and that produced great joy and contentment in my life. A good leader realizes that the success of her "disciples" reflects well on her. Indeed, her goal should be to "work herself out of a job."

HE WAS UNDER AUTHORITY HIMSELF

This last principle is the most important. One of the most dangerous temptations of a leader is thinking that she is not accountable to others. Jesus refused to fall into this trap. He stated in no uncertain terms His commitment to remain under His Father's authority and stay within His boundaries. "So Jesus answered them, 'My teaching is not mine, but his who sent me. If anyone's will is to do God's will, he will know whether the teaching is from God or whether I am speaking on my own authority. The one who speaks on his own authority seeks his own glory, but the one who seeks the glory of him who sent him is true, and in him there is no falsehood'." (John 7:16-18)

Jesus effectively led and ministered because He took His direction from a source outside Himself. He made time with His Leader His highest priority and this guided Him at every turn. If even Christ willingly placed Himself under the supervision of another, how much more should we as leaders look for wise counselors to hold us accountable and give us direction? Those who choose to "go it alone" set themselves up for failure; and when a leader falls, his failure affects countless lives. A wise leader welcomes accountability and the protection of placing himself under the authority of godly counselors.

If we are serious about obeying the Great Commission, giving our lives to sharing the gospel and discipling others in the faith, we must develop the qualities Jesus demonstrated. But do not panic. This is not as overwhelming a task as it may seem. God always provides the grace to do what He requires. I suggest you begin by making it a matter of prayer. Ask the Lord to build the characteristics of quality leadership into your life. Perhaps you would find it helpful to use the principles of this chapter as an outline. Paul writes in Philippians 4:19, "But my God shall supply all your need according to His riches in glory by Christ Jesus." (KJV) As you admit your need to grow in this area, He will surely meet you where you are and lead you to the place He longs for you to be.

God calls us to lead and disciple others whether on what looks like a large scale, as in a public ministry, or what looks like a smaller one, such as a mother training her own children. You may not feel like a leader, but remember that God has set us up for success by providing everything we need through the testimony of His Word, the example of His Son and the power of His Holy Spirit. And, "it is God who works in you, both to will and to work for his good pleasure." (Philippians 2:13) Let *Him* do the work of making you the leader He envisioned before the beginning of time and savor the blessing within these boundaries.

CHAPTER NINE

Making the Most of Inevitable Opposition

"How firm a foundation, ye saints of the Lord,
Is laid for your faith in His excellent Word!
What more can He say than to you He hath said,
To you who for refuge to Jesus have fled?

When through the deep waters I call thee to go,
The rivers of sorrow shall not overflow;
For I will be with thee, thy troubles to bless,
And sanctify to thee thy deepest distress.

The soul that on Jesus hath leaned for repose,
I will not, I will not desert to his foes;
That soul, though all hell should endeavor to shake,
I'll never, no, never, no, never forsake!"

Rippon's Selection of Hymns, 1787
Hymns for the Living Church

*D*uring my second year in Dallas I served for a few months as the interim director of EXCEL. Many mornings, my prayer time consisted of lying prostrate on the floor quoting the words of this great hymn of the faith, begging the Lord to strengthen me in the face of overwhelming responsibility, and its accompanying stress. I know now that this kind of anxiety directly affected my health, weakening my immune system and darkening my mental outlook. The promise that God will never leave me, and will in fact turn troubles to blessing, can provide grace to face many a challenge, but only if I really believe it.

We all have an inborn desire for approval and affirmation. At the end of any day, we would rather receive praise than criticism. Yet, one of the realities of the Christian life – even when we stay within our God-ordered boundaries – is pain caused by criticism, obstacles and opposition. How should I respond to critics of my faith? What response is appropriate to friends who do not understand the boundaries of my standards and convictions and who say or do things that hurt my feelings? How do I graciously handle cultural opposition from the ungodly? From what foundation do we face the inevitable? Jesus received opposition on a regular basis and warned the disciples that it would become their hallmark. John 15:20 records His admonition, "Remember the word that I said to you: 'A servant is not greater than his master.' If they persecuted me, they will also persecute you."

Two thousand years later, Christians still experience the truth of this statement. American Christians are amazingly protected from the physical persecution many of our brothers and sisters face around the world, but we should all expect to face opposition at some time or another. Opposition can be defined as "action against" or "resistance." That it originates from both within and without religious circles should not surprise us.

Jesus faced plenty of criticism, resistance and opposition from his friends, the religious establishment and the government of his day. In this chapter, we will learn how to respond to hardships and pain as blessings in disguise and to watch for God to sanctify those things that cause us the deepest distress. "We might be tempted to ask whether God can build character without suffering. That is a hypothetical question. He has not chosen to do so." (John Murray, <u>Behind a Frowning Providence</u>, p.17)

WHEN OPPOSITION ORIGINATES FROM THOSE WE LOVE

How many of us have experienced the pain of opposition or rejection from someone we know and love? Whether it comes from a simple misunderstanding with a friend or something as devastating as divorce, the pain stings and cuts its way into our hearts. During our years of ministry, our family has walked through some dark valleys of misunderstanding, poor communication and rejection. Because we moved so much as I grew up, I rarely experienced the pain of losing a friend over a misunderstanding. When I bid sad "goodbyes" as a child, the simultaneous hope of "hellos" always existed as I looked forward to making friends in our new town. Friendships that would have drifted apart died a natural death when we moved and other relationships formed to fill those voids.

I have now lived in Dallas longer than anywhere else in my life, and staying in one place more than two or three years has afforded plenty of time to walk through the dissolution of a friendship over irreconcilable differences. My experience has been nothing like the rejection Jesus endured when the Jews delivered Him to the Romans for crucifixion, but my pain sent me scurrying back to Scripture, looking for answers and hoping for a way to turn the loss of friendship and the pain of personal criticism into blessings that would draw me to the Lord.

Jesus experienced rejection and opposition early in his ministry. Mark 6 records His experience visiting His hometown to teach those who had watched Him grow up. As He shared in the synagogue, the people began to murmur and question, " 'Is not this the carpenter, the son of Mary and brother of James and Joses and Judas and Simon? And are not his sisters here with us?' And they took offense at him." (Mark 6:3) Though not a surprise, it must have hurt Jesus to look around the room at those who had known Him for years and to recognize the signs of disbelief and disdain on their faces.

Instead of forcing them to change, after sharing His message, Jesus quietly left. He did not let rejection dampen His determination to do the Father's will. He kept teaching boldly. Matthew 11:20 describes His reaction to another group, "Then he began to denounce the cities where most of his mighty works had been done, because they did not repent." This time, He confronted those who opposed His message, but He never forced Himself upon them.

Luke records another occasion when people would not even admit Him to their town. In chapter 9:51-56 a group of Samaritans refused to receive him in their village and the disciples wanted to respond to the insult by calling down fire to destroy them. Jesus rebuked them and reminded them that His purpose was not to destroy lives, but to save them. His calling did not change just because some refused to listen. Though He did not force change, He remained true to the commission of His Father.

Christ knew that many would fall away and reject His ministry: those who had learned and grown beside Him in Nazareth, those who heard the teaching and enjoyed the miracles but refused to repent, and those who would not even listen to His message. Perhaps the most poignant feelings of rejection came from those who walked closely with

Him and yet ultimately betrayed Him. In John 6:64, as many of his followers left Him, Jesus said, " 'But there are some of you who do not believe.' (For Jesus knew from the beginning who those were who did not believe, and who it was who would betray him.)"

As followers of Christ, rejection and misunderstanding should not surprise us. Responding with bitterness and anger does not demonstrate the love of Christ, and it hinders our ability to minister. We must accept the reality that we cannot force others to change. Jesus said, "This is why I told you that no one can come to me unless it is granted him by the Father." (John 6:65) When other reject us for aligning ourselves with Christ, we must trust God to change their hearts. Keeping this perspective will help us to follow the example of Christ and not overreact, even when the rejection feels so very personal and painful.

The mote and beam principle has helped our family maintain this perspective countless times when walking through difficulties in relationships. We are familiar with Jesus' admonition to those who would judge others: "Why do you see the speck that is in your brother's eye, but do not notice the log that is in your own eye? Or how can you say to your brother, 'Let me take the speck out of your eye,' when there is the log in your own eye? You hypocrite, first take the log out of your own eye, and then you will see clearly to take the speck out of your brother's eye." (Matthew 7:3-5) Though this was a well known passage to me and my family, we had to learn to apply its truths in new ways in order to resist the temptation to grow bitter when faced with opposition, whether in personal relationships or in criticisms of the work.

Let me give you an example. At one point I developed a close friendship with another young lady serving in ministry. We had our disagreements at times, but no serious qualms in our relationship, at least not that I was aware of.

After we had been friends about a year, she suddenly began to distance herself from me. We would plan outings to shop or visit over coffee, and she would cancel at the last minute, often giving reasons that sounded suspiciously like excuses to me.

I remember one evening vividly. She backed out of something, and I curled up in a western facing windowsill to watch the sunset and indulge in a little self-pity. I felt the rejection keenly and asked the Lord what He could possibly want to teach me from this painful situation. As I sat watching the bright colors of the day fade to muted pastels, the Lord reminded me of this principle. "Lauren," He seemed to say, "You are hurt because your friend missed a time of fellowship with you. But, how often do you casually brush aside your plans to spend time with me when a more attractive offer comes to you?" Ouch! As the realization of my own carelessness with the Lord in this area flashed through my mind, it shed a whole new light on my friend's offense.

From that time on, whenever she did something that hurt my feelings, I took the pain to the Lord and asked Him to show me how I had the same attitude or wrong motive in my interactions with Him or others. As I began to make this a practice, my spiritual life blossomed in whole new ways. The Lord used the rejection of this friend to draw me to Himself, reveal my own blind spots and give me the grace to repent. Now, our family makes a practice of asking one another, whenever faced with rejection or opposition, "What do we need to learn from this?" We still feel the pain, but we receive it as from the Lord and appreciate the opportunity to draw nearer to Him.

So, Jesus gives us a number of tools to use in handling hardships that originate with those we know and love. Sometimes we need to quietly leave the scene and give the Holy Spirit time to work in the hearts of others. At other times, Jesus expects us to confront the issues, but leave any persuasion to Him. Finally, we should use difficulties as springboards to explore blind spots in our own lives, looking for how we demonstrate the same unpleasant attitudes or actions in our relationship with the Lord. As we learn to consistently apply these methods, we can walk, serve and minister without the specter of bitterness or the consequences of our own anger. Learning to practice these principles when opposition comes from those we know and love will prepare us for facing it from those outside our circle of friends and acquaintances, those who do not know us, much less the God we serve.

WHEN OPPOSITION COMES FROM THE WORLD

Jesus turned bad news into blessing by letting opposition spur Him on rather than slow Him down. Matthew 14 records the final days of John the Baptist's imprisonment and then His death at the request of a foolish girl and spiteful queen. Jesus responded to the news by heading for a deserted place, presumably for time alone with the disciples. When the people heard He was in the area, they gathered in droves to hear Him speak and clamor for healing. Rather than allowing grief to consume Him, Jesus channeled His energies into ministry and later verses record the subsequent feeding of the 5,000.

At times I feel overwhelmed by the vehemence with which some cultural leaders denounce Christianity. I find it hard not to take their rejection personally and feel helpless against foes who seem so well organized and self-satisfied. King David understood this kind of opposition and wrote about it in Psalm 73. He listed the crimes of men in his culture and concluded by saying, "But when I thought how to understand this, it seemed to me a wearisome task, until I went into the sanctuary of God; then I discerned their end." (verses 16-17) David understood what Jesus knew, and what we should cling to when confronted by wickedness in our day. He continues, "Truly you set them in slippery places; you make them fall to ruin. How they are destroyed in a moment, swept away utterly by terrors!" (verses 18-19).

Learning to view criticism and opposition in light of eternity is a crucial principle for doers, because we tend to have an "It's up to me to save the world!" mentality. At times, I have wept with frustration and fatigue thinking of the enormous needs in our culture and around the world and my inability to meet them all. I cannot understand why God allows abortion, pornography, child abuse, murder, rape, and all the other sins that plague our world to seemingly rage unchecked. Surely these pained our Lord, but His faith enabled Him to trust His Father to oppose the forces of evil while He remained focused on His specific purpose and calling. He realized they fell outside of His boundaries at that time; for His people, they would be addressed at the cross. Regarding the truly wicked, Jesus foresaw their ultimate end and trusted God to deal with them rather than allowing a desire "to just do something" to distract Him from the specific job set before Him.

My natural responses to opposition from unbelievers are anger, frustration and a sense of helplessness, but Jesus demonstrated the proper response: move on with His work, and the proper emotion: pity. Unbelievers seem triumphant at times, but God has numbered their days. When their life on earth ends, they will face the results of their wicked ambitions for eternity. When viewed in this light, can we not follow Christ's example, release our anger, and channel our energies into influencing our world for good? God calls us to engage our culture for Christ and stand firm against the onslaught of evil. But the key to maintaining our hope and joy in the midst of the battle is focusing on the main thing that God has called and equipped each of us to do, and remembering that He does not expect any one person to do everything.

We see an excellent example of this concept in Nehemiah chapter three. Nehemiah returns to Jerusalem and finds the walls of the city in disarray and the Israelites unorganized and unmotivated. He rallies the people and assigns each family an area of the wall to rebuild. As each one works in his place, the wall is eventually joined together. Then in chapter four, the people encounter major resistance from the leaders of the ungodly nations in the region. Nehemiah exhorts the people not to fear, but to take turns, half standing guard with weapons unsheathed and the other half continuing the work of rebuilding. Each person had his place to work and guard and as each one served faithfully, they successfully defended the city and rebuilt the walls.

In like manner, if I faithfully serve within my boundaries, I fulfill God's call and defend my portion of the wall. I must trust God to empower others to do their part and encourage them by my example rather than feeling the need to take over their responsibility and do the whole job myself. By joyfully and faithfully doing what God calls me to do, I can successfully face the opposition of the world and appropriate the victory of Christ.

The Apostle Paul provides us with another example of properly responding to opposition in Acts 17:16-21. While in Athens, He has the opportunity to preach in the synagogue and at the Areopagus, the hill where philosophers gathered to debate their beliefs. Rather than being discouraged or demoralized by their disbelief and academic snobbery, the challenges he faced in winning people to Christ energized Paul. Like Christ, he remained faithful, even though he experienced a variety of responses to his message. Some heard and rejected the gospel outright. Others put off making a decision but at least were exposed to an alternative worldview. And some became followers of Paul and continued to listen to his teaching. Presumably, at some point, they accepted the gospel message completely and also became followers of Christ.

Paul's example gives us another principle to follow. In addition to staying focused on God's calling in our lives when overwhelmed by the vices of the world, we must not lose heart when our message garners a variety of responses. The sovereign will of God determines the results of our ministry, not eloquent preaching, effective programs or emotional pleas. God may empower these tools, but only the Holy Spirit can soften a heart hardened by sinful opposition to the truth. My tendency is to want to work harder in the face of opposition, but these examples should remind me that my more important responsibility is to pray and trust God to change hearts as He chooses.

PAINFUL PROBLEMS IN THE CHURCH

Unfortunately, painful opposition often comes, not just from friends or from an ungodly culture, but also from within the church. In Matthew 23, Jesus chastises the religious establishment, listing their failures and condemning their determination to lord their position over the common people. Their behavior revolted Him because it misrepresented the character and commandments of God. Focusing on their organized opposition and the persecution He knew would end His life could have been His undoing. Yet, in response to their injustice and blindness, Christ weeps longingly over Jerusalem saying, "O Jerusalem, Jerusalem, the city that kills the prophets and stones those who are sent to it! How often would I have gathered your children together as a hen gathers her brood under her wings, and you would not!" (verse 37) Their opposition provoked pity rather than rage for He saw the desperation of their blindness.

Some People are Impossible to Please

In Luke 7:31-34, Jesus likens the religious leaders to children at play in the marketplace who say, "To what then shall I compare the people of this generation, and what are they like? They are like children sitting in the marketplace and calling to one another, 'We played the flute for you, and you did not dance; we sang a dirge, and you did not weep.' For John the Baptist has come eating no bread and drinking no wine, and you say, 'He has a demon.' The Son of Man has come eating and drinking, and you say, 'Look at him! A glutton and a drunkard, a friend of tax collectors and sinners!' " The Pharisees and their friends refused to accept counsel from either source: John or Jesus. Rather than wasting time trying to appease them, Jesus had the wisdom and grace to walk away, understanding that those bent on criticism always find something about which to complain.

Walking away from opposition is difficult to do because, on the one hand, we want acceptance, and on the other, we naturally want others to agree when we are right. Resistance pricks our pride as well as our heart. However, when faced with those in the church who refuse to be pleased regardless of the situation, walking away is wiser than attempting to reason or debate. E.M. Bounds comments in his book The Necessity of Prayer, "The most effective preaching, is not that which is heard from the pulpit, but that which is proclaimed quietly, humbly, and consistently; which exhibits its excellencies in the home, and in the community." (p.50)

Steering Clear of Man-made Traditions

Often the greatest sources of contention in the Christian community are man-made traditions. We only have to look at a listing of churches in the phone book to see the divisions caused by differing beliefs and practices. While discussions and differences about key doctrines keep the Church healthy, more often, it seems, the debates surround issues that should pale in light of eternity. They may appear larger than life when viewed individually, but when compared to the whole of Scripture, we often find them inconsequential.

Jesus refused to be stifled by the unnecessary, and

sometimes ungodly, religious traditions and practices of His day. He cared more for people than for pretense. For example, the religious leaders chastised Him several times for His actions on the Sabbath. In Matthew 12, Jesus first proclaimed His lordship over the Sabbath and defended the disciples for snacking on corn as they walked through a field. Then to add insult to injury, as far as the religious leaders were concerned, He healed a man with a withered hand. Jesus defied their expectations to make a point. He was more concerned about healing a broken person than upholding their man-made rules.

John 5 records another instance where Jesus healed a man who had waited for years by the pool of Bethesda in hopes of someday getting to the water first when an angel stirred it with rejuvenating powers. Jesus commanded the man to take up his bed and walk away, whereupon the Jewish leaders challenged him for carrying his bed on the Sabbath. How pathetic that they so quickly criticized the man for carrying his bed rather than rejoicing in the miracle!

The blindness of the leaders and strict adherence to binding practices could have provoked anger toward God for allowing it to exist, but Jesus never allowed the callousness of others to condition His relationship with the Father. The hearts of the people lay open before Him and He boldly addressed their sin. In John 5:45-47 He says, "Do not think that I will accuse you to the Father. There is one who accuses you: Moses, on whom you have set your hope. If you believed Moses, you would believe me; for he wrote of me. But if you do not believe his writings, how will you believe my words?" When challenged by the religious leaders, Jesus exhorted them to consider the motives and intents of their hearts. He was committed to obeying the Father's will above all else; were they?

We do not have the purity of Christ in addressing man-made traditions in the church today, but we have access to the same sources of wisdom: God Himself, His written word and the testimony of the Holy Spirit. There are clearly times when love for "the weaker brother" should supercede our personal freedoms so as not to cause one for whom Christ died to stumble. But, at the same time, we must resist the ungodly, controlling spirit of the hypocrite, just as Jesus resisted the Pharisees and other misguided religious leaders of His day. Christ came to give us freedom, and God means for us to embrace grace with all its joys and privileges. We should avoid those who shackle themselves and others with traditions motivated by a desire to prove their worthiness to God or otherwise earn their salvation.

By realizing that some people are impossible to please and steering clear of man-made traditions, we can weather the storms of conflict within the church. Opposition within the Body of Christ is painful, often because we find ungodly attitudes, actions and paradigms. We expect these from unbelievers but are caught off guard when they surface in people we think should know better. As in our response to opposition or rejection from friends, we must learn to turn these unpleasantries into springboards for personal soul-searching and repentance rather than allowing them to plant seeds of bitterness in our hearts. Ultimately, we must trust in God's sovereign work to bring peace and forgiveness where there has been pain in our lives and in the lives of others.

Understanding Differing Responses to Truth and the Sovereignty of God

One of the challenges I faced early on in ministry was dealing with people who heard truth and did not seem to respond to it. Though not a form of painful opposition, differing responses provoked a similar kind of discouragement. I could not understand how a room full of people could hear the same information, and some could walk out changed while others walked out complaining, gossiping or exhibiting some other behavior that demonstrated that they completely missed the point. I have had to learn that people respond to truth in different ways, and I have to trust God for the outcomes just as Christ did.

Christ was the consummate teacher with the most important message ever given to mankind. Yet, even He saw a variety of responses to the truth He lived and died to present. The parable of the sower in Matthew 13 outlines the types of responses Christ observed. We can expect to see the same things as we labor to share the gospel and bring others to maturity in the faith.

We know four types of soil exist and these produce four different results. The hard soil "by the wayside" rejects the seed outright and birds immediately pick it off, like Satan stealing the truth from cold, dry hearts. Stony soil is the second type and this produces quick results that soon wither and die, just like those who receive the truth, but never allow it to take root and grow in their hearts. The third type of soil is thorny. Like the heart that hears the truth but cannot resist the temptations of the world and the flesh, this seed only grows until the thorns and weeds surrounding it choke off its nourishment. Christ mentions the good soil, the ready heart, last. In this soil, the seed finds room to take root, grow, and produce much fruit.

In the past, I have always focused on the soil and the seed in this parable. But I reflected recently on the person of the sower. I had become discouraged by the "opposition" I faced in the form of varying responses to presentations of truth and wondered if I was somehow failing to communicate accurately and effectively for the Lord.

He reassured me by revealing three concerns of the sower. First, am I in the right field? Do I accurately understand God's calling on my life? Perhaps the results come slowly because I am working in the wrong field, attempting to sow outside of my boundaries. If so, I need to do what I can to move to the right field.

Second, am I sowing good seed? If the results vary, it could be because the seed I am sowing is not really the true word of God. God describes His Word as powerful and unable to return void. If I continually share without result, perhaps I need to examine my heart and my message.

Finally, am I sowing properly? I tell my writing students that communication does not take place unless the reader understands what the writer is saying. It is the writer's responsibility to detail her thoughts as clearly and accurately as possible. This is also true of one who speaks or otherwise shares the message of truth with others.

If I am laboring in the right field, sowing healthy doses of the words of life, and communicating effectively, than I must learn to leave the results to God. I want positive outcomes that I can control, but this does not happen when working with people. The key to not feeling like a failure and giving in to discouragement is remembering that God determines when and if people understand His message. John 1:5 states, "The light shines in the darkness, and the darkness has not overcome it." Verses 11-13 continue the thought: "He came to his own, and his own people did not receive him. But to all who did receive him, who believed in his name, he gave the right to become children of God. Who were born, not of blood nor of the will of the flesh, nor of the will of man, but of God." John 8:43 says, "Why do you not understand what I say? It is because you cannot bear to hear my word." "Jesus said, 'For judgment I came into this world, that those who do not see may see, and those who see may become blind'." (John 9:39) God expects varying responses to truth and Jesus witnessed this firsthand. So, similar experiences should not take us by surprise.

Another truth the Lord showed me through this passage was that even with good ground, results vary. "As for what was sown on good soil, this is the one who hears the word and understands it. He indeed bears fruit and yields, in one case a hundredfold, in another sixty, and in another thirty." (Matthew 13:23) The visible results of sharing God's truth will vary greatly and this does not reflect failure on the sower's part, but rather the Father's will.

By God's grace, I believe that I have invested good seed in good ground in the lives of hundreds of young ladies during my years in Dallas. But, in His providence, they are impacting the world in different ways. Some share their talents and abilities in a public way that garners much applause. And many more are quietly changing the world through simple acts of kindness performed faithfully in their own little corner.

Sometimes Even Believers Miss the Point

Another source of possible discouragement and "opposition" arises from believers who seem to miss even the most direct explanations. In Luke 18:31-33, Jesus explains His impending trial, crucifixion, and resurrection. "And taking the twelve, he said to them, 'See, we are going up to Jerusalem, and everything that is written about the Son of Man by the prophets will be accomplished. For he will be delivered over to the Gentiles and will be mocked and shamefully treated and spit upon. And after flogging him, they will kill him, and on the third day he will rise'." This seems devastatingly clear. Then verse 34 records, "But they understood none of these things. This saying was hidden from them, and they did not grasp what was said." A few chapters later the women at the tomb remember Christ's words when reminded by the angels, but when they rush to tell the disciples what they have heard, the men still do not understand or believe what Christ has told them.

In verses 25-32 of chapter 24, Luke records the scene as Jesus appears on the road to Emmaus and talks with two disciples. Finally when they reach their destination and He breaks bread at the table with them, "... their eyes were opened, and they recognized him. And he vanished from their sight. They said to each other, 'Did not our hearts burn within us while he talked to us on the road, while he opened to us the Scriptures?' " In verses 36-49, Jesus appears to the group of disciples in Jerusalem as they huddle for safety and comfort in a locked room. Only when they see and hear Him for themselves do the frightened men believe and begin to comprehend what He has been trying to tell them all along.

These examples highlight our need for the Holy Spirit's help in understanding our circumstances and the things God desires to show us. We are helpless when left to our own intellect. They also remind us that even those closest to Jesus sometimes misunderstood him. We should not be surprised when responses vary among those we disciple and teach. This should also cause us to listen carefully to what the Lord is saying to us, lest we miss the point ourselves and perhaps lead others away from the truth.

OUR FIRM AND FAITHFUL FOUNDATION

As we have seen, opposition comes in many forms. It comes in the pain of a friend's rejection, in the resistance of an ungodly culture, and in the differences of a Church filled with people still struggling to conform to the image of Christ. The way Jesus went about His life and ministry in the midst of opposition provides a thought-provoking example for each of us to follow when facing resistance in our lives. Perhaps the most beautiful picture of responding to opposition though, is not found in Christ's earthly ministry per se, but in the eternal plan of the Father in wooing the hearts of His chosen people.

Since the Garden of Eden, humans have resisted and opposed God's plans. This did not surprise God. In His sovereignty, He knew the creation of free will would lead to conflict. He did not abandon His creation to their sinful folly, but initiated the marvelous plan of redemption through His Son, Jesus Christ. For all who receive Him, He offers full pardon for their willful opposition. And just like the shepherd, who left the 99 to find the one sheep that was lost, God pursues His chosen.

J.I. Packer has said, "The fact that only the elect are saved through the preaching of the gospel does not mean that some are shut out of the kingdom who would otherwise be in it; what it means, rather, is that some do enter the kingdom by faith, whereas otherwise none would." (God's Words, p.166) God has prepared unimaginable things for those who accept His gift of salvation and follow Him. Though He pursues those He loves, He does not override the wills of those who oppose Him. At some point He "gives them over" to the consequences of their rejection, as Paul describes in the first chapter of Romans.

This truth should help guide our reactions to the inevitable opposition we face throughout life. First, we should search our hearts and make sure we confess any resistance of our own toward God and others. Secondly, the grace of God should motivate us to extend grace to those who oppose us. Having received such a great gift, can we deny forgiveness and mercy to others? Not and maintain our right standing before God. Finally, realizing that even God limits His pursuit of those who oppose Him should give us the emotional and spiritual freedom to walk away from those who persist in opposing, rejecting or otherwise hurting us, whether they are friends or strangers. Releasing others from the pain they cause us is a key factor in maintaining our health spiritually, emotionally and even physically, and we will explore it further in the next chapter.

CHAPTER TEN

Infirmity: Friend or Fear?

"I praise you, for I am fearfully and wonderfully made.
Wonderful are your works; my soul knows it very well.
My frame was not hidden from you, when I was being
made in secret, intricately woven in the depths of the earth.
Your eyes saw my unformed substance; in your book were
written, every one of them, the days that were formed
for me, when as yet there were none of them."
Psalm 139:14-16

*B*efore my diagnosis with Multiple Systemic Exhaustion Syndrome, I had many days when I really feared I was losing my mind, my Christianity or both. I did not feel "fearfully and wonderfully made." I felt flawed. My ability to *do* defined my identity, and when my strength and energy melted away, I felt like a failure. I could read the words of Psalm 139 written above, but they held no meaning for me. My boundaries seemed to press against me on all sides, and they felt like a curse rather than a blessing.

In retrospect, I realize that somewhere along the way I bought into the "debtor's ethic," aptly defined by John Piper as " ... an impulse in the fallen human heart – all our hearts – to forget that gratitude is a spontaneous response of joy to receiving something over and above what we paid for. ... If gratitude is twisted into a sense of debt, it gives birth to the debtor's ethic – and the effect is to nullify grace ... When our virtue – toward other people, or toward God – is born out of this sense of "paying back," we are in the grip of the debtor's ethic." (Future Grace, p.32)

Gratitude became a primary motivation for my hard-driving tendencies and pursuit of perfection. I thought if I only worked hard enough, I could somehow demonstrate my gratefulness to God for all that He has given me. My works would pay Him back for the sacrifice Christ made on the cross, or at least reassure Him that He made a wise choice in choosing me. When my body wore out and I could no longer "perform" for God and others, I began to wonder what possible purpose God could still have for my life.

It was a severe mercy. Severe, in that God allowed me to get very, very sick before abruptly bringing me to the end of myself. I threw myself against my limitations for years with as much final success as trying to move a brick wall by repeatedly throwing myself into it. The illness depleted my physical stamina, diminished my capacity to understand and enjoy spiritual things, and twisted my emotional outlook on life. The diagnosis was God's mercy, the first glimmer of hope that attending to my physical needs and tuning in to my God-given design could cure the symptoms causing such suffering.

In the Appendix, I list some of the specific symptoms and give more detail about the diagnosis, because I have learned that my health problems are some of the most rampant, yet undiagnosed, in our culture today, particularly among women. In this chapter, I want us to look at how Christ interacted with the physically, emotionally and spiritually ill and at the kinds of steps we can take toward healing in each area.

I did not go into my study of how our Lord "did" ministry with a goal of looking at illness. But, I found that healing was an inescapable part of Christ's ministry and examples of His compassion for the sick permeate the gospels.

JESUS' COMPASSION FOR THE SICK

Jesus had an extraordinary compassion for the sick. Luke 7:21-22 records this snapshot of His ministry: "In that hour he healed many people of diseases and plagues and evil spirits, and on many who were blind he bestowed sight. And he answered them, 'Go and tell John what you have seen and heard: the blind receive their sight, the lame walk, lepers are cleansed, and the deaf hear, the dead are raised up, the poor have good news preached to them'." Almost everywhere He went, in addition to teaching, Jesus kindly touched the weak in their infirmities and made them whole. He realized that it could be difficult for people to receive spiritual healing from sin while their physical needs cried out for their attention. Jesus patiently tended to their illnesses rather than holding their ailments against them, as if their weakness was some kind of affront to Him.

These observations comforted me, for at times I felt ashamed of my illness, this tangible reminder of my inability to do all that I desired to do for God. From my perspective, the ability to perform determined my value as a person. When that faltered, I suddenly felt vulnerable, helpless and frustrated. Seeing Jesus' compassion with the sick throughout the gospels revealed a new aspect of His heart to me. I realize now that many heard Jesus teach, just as I "heard" through reading and studying the Scriptures. But only the sick experienced a unique measure of His power in their bodies when He touched and healed them. "And all the crowd sought to touch him, for power came out from him and healed them all." (Luke 6:19)

As I have trusted in and waited on Him for healing, I

have sensed His presence and benefited from His touch in ways I never before dreamed possible. John Piper quoted a poem in a sermon of his I heard recently and it ended with these words, "He (God) used the thorn to pin aside the veil that hides His face." I believe God gives His compassionate presence as a special gift to the weak, for they depend on Him in ways the healthy never fully understand.

Not only did Jesus personally heal the sick, when He commissioned the seventy to go and spread the good news of His coming, He gave special instructions for their dealings with the ill: "Heal the sick … and say to them, 'The kingdom of God has come near to you'." (Luke 10:9) Healing was a miraculous sign of the presence of God's kingdom. It also garnered the attention of all who witnessed it, thus opening the door for many to understand emotional and spiritual truths that are vital to lasting health and wholeness.

My pastor recently encouraged our congregation to look for Christ in the midst of every story in Scripture. He went on to point out that the parable of the Good Samaritan takes on a whole new meaning when we see Christ as the hero of the story. Like the Samaritan who showed mercy to the beaten and dying man on the roadside, Christ came to show compassion to a world full of men and women beaten and dying in their sin. In our helplessness, He picked us up and poured a healing balm on our wounds then paid for our continued restoration with His own life's blood. If He would go to such great lengths to heal our spirits, do we honestly believe He does not care for our physical infirmities? I lost sight of this in the midst of my circumstances, but now that I have slowed down enough to really listen to Him again, His compassion overwhelms me.

JESUS USED HEALING TO CHALLENGE THE STATUS QUO

Not only did Jesus use physical healing to demonstrate

His compassion for those in need, He also used it to challenge others' thinking about Him and His work. He notoriously frustrated the Pharisees and other religious leaders by healing people on the Sabbath. Luke 13:12-17 records the time he healed a crippled woman on the Sabbath, in the synagogue, in front of the religious leaders. When the leaders protested, He challenged them: "You hypocrites! Does not each of you on the Sabbath untie his ox or his donkey from the manger and lead it away to water it? And ought not this woman, a daughter of Abraham whom Satan bound for eighteen years, be loosed from this bond on the Sabbath day?" His words shamed his adversaries but caused great rejoicing among His followers. He cared much more for meeting their needs than staying within the legalistic and self-serving parameters of the priestly elite.

In Luke 14:1-6, Jesus confronts the religious hierarchy again, this time by healing a man at the home of one of the "chief" Pharisees on the Sabbath. He challenges them to show compassion for those under their spiritual care saying, "Which of you, having a son or an ox that has fallen into a well on a Sabbath day, will not immediately pull him out?" In the first example, He questioned their approach to meeting the normal physical needs of the people they led. In the second, He urged them to care for those in duress as well.

A final example shows how Jesus challenged the status quo of their thinking about those whose illnesses made them outcasts. The culture of that day viewed leprosy as a sign of God's judgment, but Jesus dealt gently with this leper: "While he was in one of the cities, there came a man full of leprosy. And when he saw Jesus, he fell on his face and begged him, 'Lord, if you will, you can make me clean.' And Jesus stretched out his hand and touched him, saying, 'I will; be clean.' And immediately the leprosy left him." (Luke 5:12-13) Jesus did not demand a spiritual revival before He touched the man; He simply healed him.

Many times, I have felt I could only come to God when I had everything together. I loved to tell him of the victories but loathed admitting the trials. My illness changed all that. I could no longer pretend – with God, or anyone else – that I had everything under control in my life. Indeed, prior to my diagnosis, I had been living a lie for years, trying to maintain a good front on the outside but inside, withering away bit by bit. In my pride, I forgot that the One who formed me in the recesses of my mother's womb understands every frailty in the form He designed.

Just recently another verse stood out to me which highlights this fallacy and the pride of thinking I could pretend with my Creator. Psalm 143:1-2 says, "Hear my prayer, O LORD, give ear to my supplications: in thy faithfulness answer me, and in thy righteousness. And enter not into judgment with thy servant: *for in thy sight shall no man living be justified.*" (KJV, emphasis mine) So many times I served and worked and poured myself out in valiant attempts to "justify" myself – or to prove to God that He made a good choice in justifying me. When I kept my problems to myself, whether health needs, emotional struggles or spiritual questions, I tried to do the impossible. By accepting the state of my health, I took the first step toward spiritual healing, because I learned that it was okay to admit my desperate need.

King David provides us with a good example of one who quickly and unashamedly poured out His needs to the Lord. In Psalm 142:1-3a he writes, "With my voice I cry out to the Lord; with my voice I plead for mercy to the Lord. I pour out my complaint before him; I tell my trouble before him. When my spirit faints within me, you know my way!" When I was overwhelmed, *then* He knew me. What a concept! I was reluctant to share my deepest heart cries with the Lord for fear of seeming ungrateful or incapable, as if my job were to balance the blessings and trials in my life and "just be grateful" for both. But, Christ came that I might throw away the scale. I see now that telling Him of my needs glorifies Him. He no more expects me to take care of myself than a father expects a five year old to meet her needs without his help.

HEALING THAT GLORIFIES GOD

To that end, sometimes God allows sickness in order to glorify himself through the life of the unhealthy person. When questioned by the disciples in John 9:3 about a man born blind, "Jesus answered, 'It was not that this man sinned, or his parents, but that the works of God might be displayed in him'." His condition was not a punishment for sin, but rather, it was an opportunity to demonstrate the powerful work of God in his life. Jesus healed him, and the man then had occasion to stand before peers and priests and testify of God's mercy in his life. Jesus' touch brought healing and gave the man an opportunity to testify of God's greatness in a way that would have been impossible had he never known blindness.

John records that when Jesus heard his friend Lazarus lingered with a deadly illness, "… he said, 'This illness does not lead to death. It is for the glory of God, so that the Son of God may be glorified through it'." (John 11:4) By delaying his visit, Jesus allowed Lazarus, and his family, to walk through the valley of the shadow of death. Yet, He did not forget or abandon them – He loved them. (John 11:35-36) He chose to delay the healing in order that a greater glory would come to his Father.

I have definitely seen this aspect of healing in my life as well. I have no doubt that God could have instantly touched and healed my maladies, but He chose not to do that. As I recover, little by little, God is teaching me lessons that I get to share with those around me. Indeed, it is for the purpose of encouraging others and hopefully sparing them from a similar fate that I set out to write down these thoughts. The personal cost of this illness has been high, but I am encouraged as I see these insights bear fruit in the lives of others; I see them benefiting from my weakness. It is a vivid illustration of God's promise that in my weakness, He is strong. In my frailty, He is my comfort, and everyone sees that. I pray that they – and you! – learn from my example and do not have to walk through the same valley. Because of the benefit to others, and myself, I can now say with confidence that I would not trade these physical "boundaries" for anything, even if that means I never fully recover. The rewards of richer intimacy with Christ far outweigh the temporary trials of weakness.

UNDERSTANDING THE SPIRITUAL SIDE OF HEALING

Learning to appreciate the treasures of intimacy found in the midst of suffering has been one of many spiritual breakthroughs in the last few years. As the Holy Spirit and the truths of Scripture permeate my heart and mind, I am experiencing renewed spiritual freedom. A significant spiritual and/or emotional breakthrough has prefaced every major step forward in my physical recovery. This highlights another part of Jesus' approach to healing: He knew a spiritual component exists in physical healing. After cleansing the lepers at their request, he tells them in Luke 17:19, "Rise and go your way; your faith has made you well." Another time he tells a blind man: "Recover your sight; your faith has made you well." (Luke 18:42)

Faith is a key to physical healing for some. Its mention here points to the reality that our spiritual state affects our physical condition. Though physical healing sometimes precedes spiritual awakening, as in the examples cited earlier, the opposite can also be true: spiritual healing may be required before the body is restored to health. And sometimes, spiritual healing occurs while the body languishes and, in God's providence, He reserves physical healing for the other side of the grave.

For me, healing has been a lengthy process. Outside of the miraculous, one rarely recovers from a chronic condition instantly. My doctors have had to remind me of this as the months stretch into years, and I am still not back to full health. Time spent resting provides quiet space for reflection, and the years of recovery have provided many opportunities for soul-searching and spiritual house cleaning. I mentioned some of Satan's lies that found their way deep into my subconscious earlier: that I was of no use to God without the ability to do, and that I was a failure because I lacked the strength required to perform at the supernatural level I had attempted to for years.

These poisons ate away at my faith and trust in God and, in addition to asking for His healing touch in my body, I have had to ask for His help in regaining the ground surrendered to Satan when I began believing his lies. When Christ takes our sins away at the point of salvation, our eternal destiny is fixed. But the process of growing in grace and battling both the flesh and the enemy of our souls continues until we enter heaven. After admonishing believers not to go to bed angry, Paul warns them in Ephesians 4:27: "Give no opportunity to the devil." This highlights an important concept in spiritual warfare: we can actually make room for Satan in our lives by resisting the grace of God. We do not lose our salvation, but we allow Satan a place of influence. Once he stakes a claim, he begins to wrap his lies around every aspect of our lives, and before long, he is entrenched.

Ephesians 6:12 tells us, "For we do not wrestle against flesh and blood, but against the rulers, against the authorities, against the cosmic powers over this present darkness, against the spiritual forces of evil in the heavenly places."

The battle is in the spiritual realm, not in the physical one that so readily claims my attentions most of the time. I must fight the enemy by employing the weapons God designed, the armor of God we discussed in Chapter Six. Though I prayed this on regularly, my sin still allowed the enemy to take up residence in areas of my soul, and I then had to go through the process of repenting and asking God to reclaim that ground.

James 4:7 says, "Submit yourselves therefore to God. Resist the devil, and he will flee from you." It took several months for me to realize that the lack of joy in my life resulted from the surrendered ground in my soul. Once I confessed that to the Lord and repented of my sin, He freed me from the enemy's bondage and gave me grace to begin recognizing and resisting his lies again. I do not believe we have the strength and power to successfully defend ourselves against the devil. He has been furthering his agenda of death and destruction since the beginning of time and only the foolish attempt to stand in his way. But, my victory is assured because of Jesus, and He will win the battles as I focus my attentions and energies on Him, praying, "And lead me not into temptation, but deliver me from evil: For *thine* is the kingdom, and the power, and the glory, forever." (Matthew 6:13, KJV)

Several months after asking God to reveal the root sins that allowed Satan's presence and take back any ground I had surrendered to his control, I learned another important step toward emotional and spiritual healing. From the time I was a child, my parents taught me that forgiveness was a choice. When a brother or sister did something that hurt my feelings and asked for forgiveness, I had to choose to forgive them, a conscious decision to no longer hold the offense against them. But just recently, I have learned that forgiveness is more than a decision of the will. It also requires releasing others from the emotional pain they cause me.

A subtle but critical difference exists here. When I choose to forgive, I make up my mind to let go of an offense. But, what do I do about the pain that remains? If someone pushes me and I fall and skin my knee, I can decide to forgive them, but my knee still stings. I may limp for days before it heals and I walk normally again. In much the same way, we all know that we can obediently choose to forgive someone who hurts us, but we do not just immediately forget the pain caused by that offense. Once a dog bites us, we never pet the dog again without the memory of the sharp pain of his teeth chomping our flesh. And when someone, particularly someone we trust, inflicts pain, it takes a long time to forget the feeling.

Before I share some simple steps that have helped me to forgive offenses and move forward in faith, let me lay some groundwork. Remember the mote and beam principle we discussed in Chapter Nine? We must keep this in mind when discussing forgiving others. Christ has forgiven our sins against Him, so we have no right to withhold forgiveness from those who sin against us. In addition, when our spiritual siblings sin against us, we must remember that Christ has already paid for their sin as well. So, forgiving fellow believers is simply agreeing with God that their debt has been sufficiently paid with the blood of Christ. To resist the grace to forgive puts us in opposition to God ... a dangerous place to be, and not one where we are likely to experience healing.

With that said, several years ago, my parents went through some counseling training by a man named John Regier followed by a conference led by a former pastor of ours who had apprenticed with John. The insights John and Bob shared are profound, yet simple, and applying them in the life of our family changed us forever. Applying them in their relationship revolutionized Mom and Dad's marriage. When they taught each of us "kids" the principles by walking us through them one at a time, our relationships were strengthened and trust deepened. These steps were vital in bringing freedom and emotional healing in my life, and it is my hope that briefly sharing them here opens doors of insight for you to explore further.

In order to experience emotional healing from the pain inflicted by others – after remembering the cross – we can do several things. The first is to identify those who caused the pain, whether they did it intentionally or not. The second step is to write out how each individual hurt us and how that made us feel. For instance, "Dad spoke harshly to me about my school assignment and that made me feel sad, not good enough, inadequate and ashamed." Or, "My husband snapped at me in front of the children and that made me feel defensive, vulnerable and unable to please him."

The third step is to explain the situation to the Lord and ask Him to heal that hurt specifically. "Lord Jesus, would you please heal the hurt in my life caused by Dad's harshness, or by my husband's criticism." The final step is to ask the Holy Spirit to bring to mind a Scripture verse, words from a spiritual song, or a picture of how Jesus heals that particular pain. In this case, He might bring to mind the verse: "The Lord is good to all: and His tender mercies are over all His works." Psalm 145:9 (KJV). This reminder of the Lord's tenderness and goodness to His own could encourage us that, regardless of the opinions of others, God looks on us with love.

As I said before, these steps are amazingly simple, yet profoundly effective. Applying them enriches our faith as we learn to agree with God about who we are in Him and to believe in the depths of forgiveness He extends to us and to those who cause us pain. Each time I go through this process, I'm humbled with the realization that I am also guilty of causing pain and in need of the forgiveness of God and others. As long as the hurt resided in my heart, I could not trust

God the way He or I desired, but by walking in obedience to God's commands to both repent and forgive, He is guiding our relationship toward a whole new level of intimacy.

I took a huge step toward freedom last summer. One evening, I felt sad and discouraged because a casual friendship with a man was not progressing the way I hoped it would. I felt anxious and upset thinking, "When will God ever bring the man I am to marry?" As I pondered this question, the Holy Spirit prompted me to think back to the last time I experienced deep pain in a relationship with a man. I then remembered an evening spent weeping in the shadows outside next to our screened-in pool as the realization sunk in that a close friend from college was not going to be my husband. I could almost feel the pieces of my heart cascading down with my tears as my dream of marriage to this man died.

I can see now that I was mourning more than one relationship that night. For as long as I could remember, I expected my life romance to turn out like my mother's. She and Dad met in college and married right out of school; I just assumed I would follow in her footsteps and marry and start a family once I finished college. God knew my dream. When it did not come true, I decided I could not trust Him in this area, and ever since then, I was anxious about finding a spouse. I wondered about each man I met, "Could this be the one?" and after a little interaction would begin envisioning how my life calling would mesh with his and how I would fit into his family. As I pondered this sequence, I realized that I needed to ask God to heal the pain caused by the relationship from college, along with that caused by others I had known through the years. My mother prayed through the hurts with me, and I experienced a new freedom in my spirit.

I believe that freedom then allowed me to see the deeper cause of my pain. At the core of the issue was sin, specifically my anger toward God for not leading me in the paths of my choosing. Marriage at the age of 22 was not His plan for me, and I felt betrayed, frustrated and alarmed that His direction for my life differed from mine. Admitting that was hard. Who wants to tell the Lord, "I'm really upset with YOU!"? I certainly didn't, but once I humbled myself to admit the obvious, His forgiveness and grace immediately flooded my soul and put the pieces of my heart back together.

Since that time, I have had a marvelous contentment regarding the area of marriage. More importantly, a return to right believing enabled me to trust God more deeply. This is the goal of healing the hurts: that nothing hinders our vision of who God really is. The Scriptures are full of a beautiful, majestic, awe-inspiring glimpse of our God, and we should refuse to allow our pain – or anything else – to hinder us from pursuing Him.

LEARNING TO ABIDE

The spiritual, emotional and physical process of healing is just that, a process. I have not recovered overnight and slow progress and occasional setbacks have provided rich opportunities for reflection and deepening intimacy with God. I had many things to learn through this time, but perhaps one of the most important was that the illness was a *consequence*, not a *punishment*. God did not simply allow this into my life because of my sin, though He could have. Allowing stress, anxiety, and fear to consume my thoughts and destroy my peace was certainly an affront to God. But, rather than a punishment, I see the illness as a tool that God chose to use in drawing me to Himself and giving me a deeper message to encourage others. I have learned that He still values me, and I am no less important just because I can no longer do all I did before my health failed. In some ways this has seemed to narrow my boundaries, but in other ways, the boundaries have been greatly enlarged.

Christ says in John 15:2, "Every branch of mine that does not bear fruit he takes away, and every branch that does bear fruit he prunes, that it may bear more fruit." I have experienced in the flesh the pain of pruning. Amazingly enough, some of my most effective ministry has occurred during my recovery, even though the time I have spent with people has been halved, at least. Learning from the pain and passing on the lessons by word and example multiplies the effectiveness of the time I do spend with others.

An abiding branch bears fruit effortlessly. In like manner, as I learn to abide in Christ, the aroma of ministry wafts naturally to those around me. It is not conjured but rather escapes to leave its mark on those touched by a word, gesture, or expression. "Abide in me, and I in you. As the branch cannot bear fruit by itself, unless it abides in the vine, neither can you, unless you abide in me. I am the vine; you are the branches. Whoever abides in me and I in him, he it is that bears much fruit, for apart from me you can do nothing." (John 15:4-5)

During my first ten years of ministry, I became increasingly busy about the Lord's work and increasingly unwilling to abide at His feet, soaking up the grace and strength to do His work. My illness slowed me down enough to learn to rest in Him again. A severe mercy, yes, but a blessing I would not trade.

Jesus' words to Martha, as He met with her after Lazarus died, provide comfort for me as well. He told her, "I am the resurrection and the life. Whoever believes in me, though he die, yet shall he live, and everyone who lives and believes in me shall never die. Do you believe this?" (John 11:25-26) My hope is in Christ ... do I truly believe his promise? After walking with Him through the valley of infirmity these many months, the answer is a resounding "Yes!" These trials are my own precious boundary lovingly set by my sovereign Father, and I no longer reject them as fears but embrace them as friends. In the words to her song, "Thank You for this Thorn," Twila Paris sings, "I never thought I'd say it without reservation, But I am truly grateful for this piercing revelation … I thank You. Really, I thank You, for this thorn." Amen.

CHAPTER ELEVEN

The Blessing of Boundaries

"Things that once were wild alarms
cannot now disturb my rest;
Closed in everlasting arms, pillowed on the loving breast.
O, to lie forever here, doubt and care and self resign,
While He whispers in my ear, I am His, and He is mine."
George. W. Robinson

Throughout this book, we have defined boundaries as limitations, outlines, or borders that mark an end or a beginning. Through my illness, the Lord showed me the limits, or the boundaries, of my physical endurance. He also used the illness to expand the limits of my understanding of myself and of Him. Our culture scoffs at boundaries in many ways, but God intends for them to free and bless, not fetter or bind, His children. Accepting them enables us to begin a glorious journey with Christ inside the parameters for our lives that He established to bless us even before He founded the world.

Ephesians 2:10 says, "For we are his workmanship, created in Christ Jesus for good works, which God prepared beforehand, that we should walk in them." At one time, each of us followed "the course of this world, ... the prince of the power of the air, the spirit that is now at work in the sons of disobedience." (Ephesians 2:2) We were bound by Satan and limited by His power, ever fulfilling the desires of the flesh as those who were by nature destined for wrath. (Ephesians 2:3) But God, in His great mercy, picked us out of the enemy's pasture and enveloped us into his flock, giving us new borders in which to experience all the spiritual blessings He has prepared for us in Christ. (Ephesians 1:3) Considered this way, each of us should welcome the boundaries of our lives. God designed these to bless us "exceedingly abundantly above all that we ask or think." (Ephesians 3:20, KJV) Indeed, "Eye hath not seen, nor ear heard, neither have entered into the heart of man, the things which God hath prepared for them that love Him." (I Corinthians 2:9, KJV)

GOD DESIRES A RETURN ON HIS INVESTMENT

God desires faithfulness in our appointed areas of jurisdiction. Before faithfulness must come awareness. We cannot function within the boundaries if we do not know they exist. I am not talking about following the commands of Christ or obeying the whole of Scripture; that is a given. I am talking about discerning the will of God for my life through understanding the special verses of Scripture He impresses upon my heart, the talents and abilities He has given me, and the times in which I live. Matthew 24:46 says, "Blessed is that servant whom his master will find so doing when he comes." It is reasonable and appropriate for God to expect us to fulfill His will for our lives. We have all of Scripture and the Holy Spirit to guide us in the right path. And it behooves us to work diligently: "Watch therefore, for you know neither the day nor the hour" when the Lord will return or call you home to heaven. (Matthew 25:13)

I can only say this after building the case for boundaries

in the preceding chapters. Were the admonition to work given first, all the doers would use that to justify their doing! I know, for this was my misguided focus for many years. The key to enjoying the blessing of boundaries is discerning the will of God and doing *all but only* that which He calls and enables us to do. Jesus taught the disciples to ask for their daily bread, what they needed for sustenance, one day at a time. I am learning to pray that way for grace and strength as well by modifying Paul's words in Ephesians 4:7, "Lord, please allow me to accept the full measure of grace you offer me today, through Christ, to accomplish Your will."

The most exciting benefit of knowing and flourishing within God-ordained boundaries is the knowledge that, in doing so, we glorify God. As we glorify Him, we fulfill our highest, holiest and most important purpose in life. God delights in watching His children realize their potential in much the same way that parents delight in watching their children succeed, each in their own unique area of giftedness. Just as parents hope and pray for a return on their investment in piano lessons, art lessons, dance, drama, speech, writing or any other area of training, God desires a return on His investment of talents, gifts and abilities in His children. By finishing every part of His work on earth, Jesus faithfully fulfilled the sum total of His Father's will for his life.

Jesus tells the story in Luke 19:11-27, of a nobleman who left his home for a journey. During his final briefing for the servants he intended to leave behind, he gave them each ten pounds with the admonition to "Engage in business till I come." While he was away, the servants did different things with their trusts. Two of them invested the money in ventures that produced dividends, one doubling their money, and the other earning a 50% profit. The third servant hid the money and waited for the master's return. When he came home, the nobleman called each man to account for his use of the ten pounds. He praised those who multiplied the money and rewarded them according to their profits, but he harshly judged the one who hid the money away and did nothing with it.

The lesson for us is clear. God entrusts each of us with abilities, talents and gifts, and He expects us to use them for His glory. But, we have a choice. We can hide these away and harbor them for ourselves, or we can multiply them by using them for God and others. There may be seasons where our ability to invest time and energy into multiplying our visible assets for the Lord varies. But, my prayer is that I will consistently and faithfully maximize my potential, always moving toward the goal of God's glory, regardless of the pace. When God calls me to account for my life, I want to hear the words Matthew recorded in a similar parable, "Well done, good and faithful servant. You have been faithful over a little; I will set you over much. Enter into the joy of your master." (Matthew 25:21)

The challenge in this, particularly for the doer, is not to get so carried away with wanting to fulfill our calling in life that our desire eclipses our commitment to God's glory. Glorifying and enjoying Him must remain our highest goal, even more important than what we think we can accomplish. One of the boundaries He designed to bless us is the command to glorify Him above all else. By His grace, it should keep us from getting sidetracked by all the cares of the world that constantly clamor for our attention. I love John Piper's observation: "God is most glorified in us when we are most satisfied in Him." (Desiring God) Satisfaction grows as we learn to know Him more through spending time at His feet reading and praying through His Word.

Putting God's glory first is the key to maximizing His investment in us and enjoying His blessings. And, one of the mercies of God is that He does not reserve all of these blessings for heaven. We enjoy many of them now as we walk in His will, fulfilling the calling He designed for each of our lives. This helps to balance the suffering and opposition destined to confront us along the way. When our family decided to make the move to Dallas, I had mixed feelings about leaving our church, saying goodbye to friends, and giving up our home. One of the passages God used to encourage me during that time was Luke 18:29-30, "Truly, I say to you, there is no one who has left house or wife or brothers or parents or children, for the sake of the kingdom of God, who will not receive many times more in this time, and in the age to come eternal life."

LIVING WITH THE INEVITABLE

Although we need to learn to see all of life as an opportunity to minister, we must maintain balance and understand the physical limitations God has built into our bodies. And, we must not become so zealous in seeing and meeting needs that we unintentionally begin to take on more than God intends. Jesus did not heal every person living in Israel during His lifetime. He did not fix the political problems with Rome. I believe Christ accepted that, in God's providence, some areas of concern never change completely this side of heaven. For instance, He grieved over Israel's refusal to repent in Luke 13:34-35, but He knew they were not going to budge and did not exhaust Himself trying to change their stubborn hearts.

In another passage He makes a statement that seems harsh at first. When the disciples criticize the woman who anointed Him with costly perfume for not spending the money on the poor, Jesus replies, "The poor you always have with you, but you do not always have me." (John 12:8) A reasonable application for our times seems to be that God does not call us to exhaust ourselves trying to do something He has already said will not be accomplished this side of eternity. Feeling the responsibility to alleviate the suffering of all those starving around the world is not within the boundaries of God's call on our lives. This does not mean we do nothing. But, and I'm speaking as a doer here, it does not mean I am a failure for not being able to physically do everything.

Speaking as a recovering perfectionist, living with the inevitable also means I do not have to stress myself out reaching for perfection in the Christian walk. Now, each of us has a responsibility to follow Christ, listen to the lessons the Holy Spirit teaches us through the Word, and walk in a manner worthy of the Father, but we will not attain perfection this side of heaven. It is God's responsibility, as the One who begins the work of redemption in each heart, to complete the process of sanctification in His time. Philippians 1:6 says, "Being confident of this very thing, that *He which hath begun a good work in you will perform it* until the day of Jesus Christ;" (KJV, emphasis mine) I can be confident that God will do His work of perfecting in my life in His way and in His time. I must leave the burden of that responsibility with Him rather than trying to carry it on my shoulders and bearing the fruit of disappointment and discouragement.

This is one of the most important boundaries to learn to recognize: where my responsibility stops and where God's begins. Looking back, I realize that much of my stress and exhaustion arose from feeling responsible for cares and concerns resting in God's jurisdiction, not mine. I used to think, "My shoulders are not broad enough for this responsibility!" It took a long time to realize that God was saying "Yes, that's right ... but Mine are." When I was finally able to release this area into God's hands, I could then imagine the joys described by the hymnwriter, George W. Robinson: "Things that once were wild alarms cannot now disturb my rest; Closed in everlasting arms, pillowed on the loving breast. O, to lie forever here, doubt and care and self resign, While He whispers in my ear, I am His, and He is mine."

IMPLEMENTING THE "PASSIVE" COMMANDS OF CHRIST

If we focus on working as the means of ministering to each person who crosses our path, we will quickly expend our energy. Often the things God commands are more passive physically but stringent spiritually, such as "believe on Him (Jesus) whom He (God) hath sent." Grasping this truth revolutionized my perspective on ministry. Implementing the "passive commands" of Christ changed who I *was*, and that change enabled deeper and more effective ministry to flow naturally to those around me.

Let me give you an example. A year or so ago, I took a couple of days for a mini-retreat and went to stay in the home of a friend who was out of town. The time alone provided an opportunity for rest and relaxation, as well as some long, uninterrupted time with the Lord. I was reading through Psalms at the time, and the first morning I found myself at Psalm 37. Particularly since this passage was so familiar to me, I prayed before reading it, "Holy Spirit, would you please show me something new here!" Then as I began reading, I made a list of things in the psalm that God said were my responsibility, and those that were His.

After making my list, the first thing I noticed was that God's responsibilities far outnumbered mine. The second thing I observed was that most of the things God expected from me were "passive," meaning, they related to a state of *being* rather than *doing*. Throughout the psalm, God admonishes us to trust Him, delight in Him, commit our ways to Him, rest in Him and wait patiently for Him. All of these relate much more to decisions of the mind, will and emotions than to physical actions. The things God does instruct us to do in this psalm include the following: show mercy, give, do good, dwell in His presence forever, speak words of wisdom, talk about God's judgment, keep His ways and observe the example of the upright. Even these action statements require more of a state of mind than physical activities, though actions certainly spring from how we think and feel.

After compiling my list of responsibilities, I went back and looked at things God instructs me *not* to do. These include fretting, envy, anger, wrath, committing evil works and evil in general. This helped me to realize that some of my thoughts and feelings violated God's commands for my life. II Corinthians 10:4 tells us that "The weapons of our warfare are not carnal, but mighty through God to the pulling down of strongholds." (KJV) So, indulging in the emotions of anger, frustration, anxiety and stress meant handling the carnal weapons of my enemy. God says that our weapons are *not carnal*, but rather are emotions such as the fruit of the Spirit: "love, joy, peace, patience, kindness, goodness, faithfulness, gentleness, and self-control." (Galatians 5:22-23)

We are not to spend energy feeling angry and upset about things that only God can change. Those emotions do nothing to change the situation, but rather feed our flesh and drain our energy, leaving us unfit to serve and unfocused on God's plan. These negative emotions are the weapons of the enemy, Satan, and the believer should never try to use them. When we do, we violate God's boundaries, and we are destined to fail. Victory over the flesh, the world and the devil will only come from employing God's strategy, which exists in stark contrast to Satan's tactics.

I find it helpful to remember that God's words in Philippians 4:6 are a command, not a suggestion: "Do not be anxious about anything, but in everything by prayer and supplication with thanksgiving let your requests be made known to God." Anxiety is both a sin and a tool of the enemy. Prayer and thanksgiving should be our weapons of choice against it. When we rest within these boundaries and faithfully fulfill the things God calls us to accomplish, we will walk in joy and gratefulness rather than fear, anxiety and stress.

The parameters of responsibility God establishes for his people in Psalm 37 require obedience, which is itself a "passive" decision of the will that works itself out in what we do, how we live. "If you keep my commandments, you will abide in my love, just as I have kept my Father's commandments and abide in his love. These things I have spoken to you, that my joy may be in you, and that your joy may be full." (John 15:10-11) Obeying Christ's commands will bring us the greatest imaginable joy. We must not bite into the lie of Satan that boundaries exist to diminish our pleasure, but instead remember that, just as He did for Adam and Eve, God established these boundaries to bless us and increase our joy.

DAILY FAITHFULNESS PREPARES US FOR OUR DEFINING MOMENTS

Faithfully practicing the "passive" commands transforms us into the people God envisioned before time began. The discipline of "being" who He designed us to be also prepares us for defining moments when He does call us to *do* the spectacular. Esther's life portrays this principle. A lovely young woman, she was chosen to assume the role of queen opposite one of the most terrible tyrants who ever ruled. Apparently, her quiet spirit and outward beauty won the king's heart and vaulted Esther into the lap of luxury, and a world of intrigue.

What did queens do in those days? We know Esther spent a full twelve months in a spa-like setting with pampering designed to enhance her appeal to the king. To the casual observer, this certainly seems like a luxurious, unproductive way to spend a year. But, in those days of preparation, Esther exhibited an extraordinary spirit, one that set her apart and garnered the favor of the "keeper of the women." Esther 2:9 records, "And the young woman pleased him and won his favor. And he quickly provided her with her cosmetics and her

187

portion of food, and with seven chosen young women from the king's palace, and advanced her and her young women to the best place in the harem."

Once Esther was crowned queen, she moved to her new quarters in the palace. We have no record of how she filled her days, but we can assume she continued to exhibit faithfulness in *being* the kind of woman that attracted even a horrible heathen king. When Mordecai warned her of the plight of her people, the Jews, and instructed her to plead for their lives, her defining moment came and she rose to the occasion. She took three days to fast and pray about their predicament before taking her life into her hands and going to the king.

We know how the story ends. The king accepts her invitation to a banquet, two days in a row. When she reveals her heritage and pleads for her people, he responds by rising to her defense and ordering the execution of her arch enemy, Haman. After the crisis passes, little more is said, anywhere in Scripture, about Esther. Though she was a woman of influence with the king and her cousin Mordecai, the Scripture does not record any more great deeds. Yet, we do not think of her life as wasted because she only once "came to the kingdom for such a time as this," do we? Of course not! She is one of the great heroines of the Christian faith. God defined her boundaries and she flourished within them.

We know the heroes – and heroines – of faith for the highlights of their lives, but their ability to shine in those moments came from faithfulness during the lifetime of daily ups and downs they most certainly experienced. God does not call us to "save the world" every day, any more than He did them. He desires consistency and promises "A faithful man will abound with blessings." (Proverbs 28:20) Doers tend to have grandiose visions of greatness for God, but the daily triumphs of faithfulness are what shape a legacy worth emulating.

LEAVING THE PHYSICAL CARES FOR THE WORLD WITH CHRIST

Daily faithfulness during the first thirty years of His life prepared Christ for His years of "full-time ministry." As He grew, He surely felt the burden of living within the confines of the flesh, surrounded by the consequences of the sins of the world. "For we do not have a high priest who is unable to sympathize with our weaknesses, but one who in every respect has been tempted as we are, yet without sin." (Hebrews 4:15) After His triumphal entry into Jerusalem, when facing the people for the last time, He remarked, "Now is my soul troubled: and what shall I say? Father, save me from this hour: but for this cause came I unto this hour." (John 12:27) At this point, the consistent communication with His Father and walking within the boundaries of God's call on His life readied Christ for His defining moment when His humiliation culminated on the cross.

Christ suffered as He carried the weight of His mission throughout His life on earth, but the burden of His passionate concern for the world intensified "in His body" as He passed through Gethsemane and went on to the cross. His suffering in the Garden was exquisite as the weight of all the purposes of God fell upon Him. Luke records, "And being in an agony he prayed more earnestly; and his sweat became like great drops of blood falling down to the ground." (Luke 22:44) His agony only increased as He endured the trial, the mocking, the beating, and the torture of the cross, all while the weight of sin and judgment crushed Him.

Jesus bore the horrific weight of our sin during His life and God's judgment of that sin in His death. Because He paid the full price, I do not have to try to carry any part of that load for myself or for others. Mercifully, God has placed a boundary around those things we can change and the emotions He wants us to entertain. I used to think it was noble to allow concern for the world to overwhelm me. I felt

I demonstrated some measure of extraordinary care and responsibility by lamenting over the pain I saw. Only when I lost my health did I internalize the truth: God never intended for me to carry the weight of the world. Jesus already died for these cares; God does not require physical death of me too.

THE CERTAINTY OF DEATH TO SELF

On the other hand, God does call His people to die to self. Again, the words of John: "He must increase, but I must decrease." (John 3:30) And, "the servant is not greater than his master..." (John 13:16, KJV) "Verily, verily I say unto you, Except a corn of wheat fall into the ground and die, it abideth alone; but if it die, it bringeth forth much fruit. He that loveth his life shall lose it; and he that hateth his life in this world shall keep it unto life eternal." (John 12:24-25, KJV) God beckons us to live within the boundaries of death to self whether our natural tendency is to race or stroll through the path of life He sets before us.

In the first chapter, I wrote of the dilemma: given the calling of God on my life, do I belong to Him gratefully, or grudgingly? To be gratefully His requires an acceptance of this principle of life from death. As I die to the flesh, His life is born in me. As I die to my own desires, and thus lay down my life for others, hopefully His life is born also in them. "Greater love has no one than this, that someone lays down his life for his friends." (John 15:13)

Dying to self occurs in different ways for different people. For me, remaining single into my thirties has required a measure of dying to my natural desires for a husband, home and children. Many of the young women I teach tell me that they pray I would marry soon. "But," I remind them, "if I had married when I thought it was time, I never would have met you. I wouldn't want to trade our time together and what God has in store here for short-sighted plans of my own." I know when I have finished the initial investment in the number of women God ordained before the foundations of the world, He will move me on to "the next thing" be that marriage or some other ministry. But, looking back over all He has allowed me to do, I would not trade my experiences for any of the smaller dreams I used to dream. His have proved so much greater and grander than mine; I would never choose to second-guess Him now.

I imagine that Christ, our expectant Bridegroom, must have this same spirit. What bridegroom does not long for his bride, eagerly counting the hours until they are one in the sight of God and man? Surely the long wait requires patience for our Lord as he listens for the signal from His Father to go get His beloved Church. Hear the heart-cry of the Lover of our souls: "In my Father's house are many rooms. If it were not so, would I have told you that I go to prepare a place for you? And if I go and prepare a place for you, I will come again and will take you to myself, that where I am you may be also." (John 14:2-3)

As much as we long for the consummation of our heavenly union with Christ, would we wish, for our sake, that He had received his Bride sooner? No, for that would mean those living now were lost to eternity. Just as we are grateful that He waited within the Father's boundaries for us, so I should gratefully wait for Him to send a bridegroom for me. I do not want to miss out on the lessons, nor shortchange those in whom He desires me to invest.

Jesus says in John 13:34, "A new commandment I give to you, that you love one another: just as I have loved you, you also are to love one another." Love defines the life of a true and mature disciple. An immature disciple can set a superficial example and admonish others to follow. A mature follower of Christ motivates her disciples by love, and love flows freely from a life full of gratitude and joy. It requires no effort and does not sap energy. It springs forth to others as naturally as breathing and can no sooner stop than one's heartbeat. When loving others becomes an effort, I have lost my connection with the source of love.

I violated God's boundaries for my life and ministry through overdoing and stubbornly striving for perfection, and I lost my connection to the Supreme Source of love. But, now that I am learning to bask in the blessings found within His boundaries, love for Him bubbles through me once again. I look forward to our times of fellowship, in the morning, and throughout the day. In our quiet times together, He feeds me, filling me up so that ministry to others spills out naturally. It is no longer a job but a lifestyle.

"His forever, only His; who the Lord and me shall part? Ah, with what a rest of bliss Christ can fill the loving heart! Heav'n and earth may fade and flee, first-born light in gloom decline; But while God and I shall be, I am His and He is mine." To these words by George Robinson I can only add, "Amen." I am ever so grateful to be His, and I pray you are too.

Appendix

WHAT IS "MULTIPLE SYSTEMIC EXHAUSTION SYNDROME?"

As I mentioned before, I want to briefly explain my physical illness in more detail in the hopes that some of you will recognize symptoms in yourselves, or in those you love, and seek help before reaching the state I did. Most of the medical information contained in this section comes from the books <u>Prescription for Nutritional Healing</u> by Balch and Balch and <u>Tired of Being Tired</u> by Hanley and Deville.

My doctor made up the title, "Multiple Systemic Exhaustion Syndrome" to cover the list of six conditions he diagnosed: adrenal exhaustion, thyroid exhaustion, hypoglycemia, chronic fatigue, systemic bacterial infections and hormonal imbalance. Let me define each of these briefly and then address more specifically the condition I feel lies at the root of all the others.

Adrenal Exhaustion

The adrenal glands are small organs that rest on each kidney. They control the production of hormones in the body: cortisone, cortisol, aldosterone, androstenedione and dehydroepiandrosterone (DHEA), adrenaline and norepinephrine. Before all the big words turn you off, let me explain in layman's terms. The adrenals essentially regulate energy by producing the four major stress hormones used by the body. They are designed to give us energy to respond to stress and other crises, like "flight or fight" scenarios. When a person lives with increased stress all the time, whether good – like battling traffic to meet a friend for dinner – or bad – like worrying about meeting a deadline or a conflict with a family member – the adrenal glands become exhausted.

In <u>Tired of Being Tired</u>, Hanley and Deville quote Dr. Aristo Wojdani, the director of the Immunosciences Laboratory in Los Angeles: "Stressful, sad and scary experiences have been shown to suppress immune function for twenty hours after the experience." (p.267) Balch and Balch write, "Stress is viewed as a psychological problem, but it has very real physical effects. The body responds to stress with a series of physiological changes that include increased secretion of adrenaline, elevation of blood pressure, acceleration of heartbeat, and greater tension in the muscles." (p.647) So, any negative experiences or emotions, especially those sustained over time, will cause physical reactions with the potential to affect profound changes in the body.

Symptoms of adrenal problems include weakness, lethargy, dizziness, headaches, memory problems, food cravings, allergies, and blood sugar disorders. (Balch and Balch, p.129) God designed the adrenals to give us an extra lift during intense moments, but He never intended for us to live in a state that required the full-time production of these "flight or fight" hormones. Hanley and Deville say, "Highly ambitious people tend to love the adrenaline rush, risk-taking, and rising to challenges." (p.7) This is why perfectionistic go-getters often suffer adrenal exhaustion.

Thyroid Exhaustion

The thyroid works in conjunction with the adrenals and helps to control the metabolism. It can get out of balance in two ways: hyperthyroidism, where too much thyroid hormone is produced, or hypothyroidism, where not enough of the hormone is produced. I was diagnosed with hypothyroidism.

Symptoms of hypothyroidism include fatigue, loss of appetite, inability to tolerate cold, a slow heart rate, weight gain, heightened symptoms of PMS, fertility problems, muscle weakness and cramping, dry and scaly skin, hair loss, recurring infections, migraines, depression and difficulty concentrating. (Balch and Balch, p.446 and 451)

A Simple Self Test

A simple way of testing the thyroid and adrenals is to take your temperature first thing in the morning, before getting out of bed, and the last thing before going to bed at night. If your temperature is 97.6 or lower in the morning, this may indicate that the thyroid is not working properly. By taking my temperature for several mornings in a row, it quickly became obvious that my body was not producing enough of the thyroid hormone needed to promote good health. For some reason, I never understood that a *low* temperature signaled as much of a health crisis as a *high* temperature. I think I thought a low temperature was a good thing, in the same way that being *under*weight might seem more advantageous to some than being *over*weight. It took a while to shift my paradigm and understand that this was a serious problem.

Another pattern I noticed was that my temperatures were often lower at night. When I discussed this with my doctor, he told me that probably indicated that I spent more energy on those days than my body produced. In other words, the adrenals were not keeping up with the demands I placed on them any more than the thyroid.

Hypoglycemia

Hypoglycemia is the medical term for abnormally low

blood sugar. Most of the time, this occurs when the pancreas secretes too much insulin as it processes food. Simply put, insulin transports glucose, or sugar, into the bloodstream to provide energy to the body. When the sugar in the blood gets out of balance, stress hormones, such as adrenaline and cortisol (produced by the adrenal glands) kick in to prevent the levels of blood sugar from dropping too much.

Symptoms of hypoglycemia include fatigue, dizziness, inability to concentrate, headaches, irritability, depression, anxiety, cravings for sweet foods, confusion, constant hunger and insomnia.

The authors of <u>Prescriptions for Nutritional Healing</u> have this to say about the increasing prevalence of hypoglycemia among Americans: "More and more Americans today may have this condition, due to poor dietary habits that include eating large quantities of simple carbohydrates, sugars, alcohol, caffeine, and soft drinks, and insufficient amounts of complex carbohydrates. High stress levels are believed to be a contributing factor in the increasing incidence of hypoglycemia." (Balch and Balch, p.448)

Chronic Fatigue

Chronic Fatigue may be defined as "a characteristic and complex array of symptoms that may mimic other illnesses." (Balch and Balch, p.286) For me, chronic fatigue meant that I was tired all the time, regardless of how many hours I slept each night. Other symptoms included aching muscles and joints, anxiety, depression, difficulty concentrating, poor memory, headaches, intestinal problems and pain, irritability, environmental sensitivities – such as when heavy perfumes cause a headache – loss of appetite, nasal congestion, recurring yeast infections and sleep disorders. (p.286-287)

This unpleasant condition is difficult to diagnose, and in my reading, I encountered countless testimonies of those whose doctors told them these symptoms were just in their heads. In other words, finding a sympathetic doctor can be a challenge.

Systemic Infections

I did quite a bit of reading about chronic, systemic yeast infections and was fairly certain they also contributed to my condition. My doctor ordered some tests which came back negative for yeast, but positive for pervasive bacterial and fungal infections in my intestinal tract. As I understand it, all kinds of bacteria, yeast and fungi live in our bodies all the time. A functioning immune system fights and kills them before they multiply to unhealthy proportions. Because my immune system was compromised, these unwanted guests were out of control.

Symptoms of intestinal infections may include constipation, diarrhea, abdominal pain, headaches, memory loss, mood swings, muscle and joint pain, sore throat, PMS, extreme fatigue, depression, hypothyroidism and adrenal problems. (Balch and Balch, p.263)

If you think you might be suffering from chronic yeast infections, I would highly recommend you take the time to read The Yeast Connection and the Woman, by William Crook, M.D. Although I was not diagnosed with a yeast infection, I found it very helpful.

Hormonal Imbalance

The final condition my doctors diagnosed was not a surprise. Hormone imbalances go right along with the other conditions listed above. Because the immune system and lymphatic systems were compromised, my body no longer produced the proper amounts of estrogen and progesterone. This caused irregular menstrual cycles and heightened symptoms of PMS. It is possible to supplement with natural hormones, but this kind of imbalance is more likely to be a symptom rather than the root cause of a chronic illness.

The Root Cause: My Hypothesis

You may have noticed that many of the conditions listed have overlapping symptoms. That made them harder to diagnose and treat without a doctor's care. I was fortunate that, when I reached the end of my rope, the Lord led us to doctors who understood these types of chronic conditions, believed they were real – not just in my head – and knew how to treat them. My desire was to use the most natural methods possible to recover, so we limited the number of prescription medications and sought to supplement with herbs and vitamins, lots of rest and a reduced workload. Slowly but surely, my body is responding. Balch and Balch do an excellent job of outlining treatment plans for each of these ailments, and if you think you may have one or more of them, I strongly encourage you to purchase their book <u>Prescriptions for Nutritional Healing</u>. It is available at many health food stores, and of course, can be found online or through a local bookstore.

For many months, it was hard to determine which conditions caused which conditions. Once my immune system was compromised, one thing led to another and many parts of my health were affected. Now that I have done some research and can look back on the months of recovery, I believe that adrenal and thyroid exhaustion were the roots of the problems for me. One of the most helpful books I read is entitled, <u>Tired of Being Tired</u>, by Jesse Lynn Hadley, M.D. and Nancy Deville. The authors state, "Adrenal fatigue affects all the interconnected systems of the body and creates a biological domino effect that causes fatigue, cravings, weight gain, mood swings, and many of the health problems people are grappling with today." (p.13)

If you recognize yourself in the lists of symptoms listed above, I would highly recommend that you purchase this book for yourself, or check it out at your local library. Hadley and Deville do an excellent job of describing adrenal exhaustion in layman's terms and provide ten "simple solutions" for restoring health. These authors also caution: "It is typical of someone who loves the adrenaline rush to maintain a level of denial about what they are doing to themselves as their inner world begins to collapse." (p.14) *Don't make this mistake!*

Suggestions to Start You on the Road to Recovery

It is not my intent to suggest a road to recovery for others. Experts with much more skill and experience should help each person develop a workable plan for restoring their health. But, let me quickly summarize a few simple steps from <u>Tired of Being Tired</u> that would apply to just about everyone, in whatever stage of health you find yourself.

1. Balance your blood sugar by eating five or six small meals a day instead of the standard three. When you maintain the proper level of sugar in the blood, energy remains constant throughout the day and the adrenals are not called to "come to the rescue" by making up with adrenaline what the body lacks in glucose.

2. Exercise, but do not work out so long and hard that you use more energy than your body has to give. If you are exhausted, gentle exercise may help, but a hard workout will just cause a greater deficit. This was quite revealing for me, because I regularly jogged, walked and taught aerobics before my health declined. I knew exercise was good for the body, but did not consider that I might be further depleting an already overtaxed system.

3. The authors encouraged me to learn to relax, get more sleep, take more time for myself and – here's

the key – refuse to feel guilty for taking care of myself. I used to feel that taking care of myself was a luxury, pampering that wasted time and money. But I am learning that I need to make time for myself, time to enjoy the life that God has given me, rather than filling every moment with frenetic "doing."

The Blessing of Boundaries

QUESTIONS AND IDEAS
FOR FURTHER STUDY

Introduction – Defining Boundaries
1. Memorize Ephesians 2:10.
2. What does it mean to do "all but only" the will of God for your life?
3. Brainstorm additional examples of the principle of boundaries found in Scripture.
4. What is the author's main premise?
5. Why is it important for the complacent to understand the blessing of boundaries? Why is it important for doers to understand?
6. Why is it critical to balance who we are and what we do? Which part of this equation is emphasized by the American culture?

Chapter One – Boundaries: Blessing or Curse?
1. Do you have a personal relationship with God through the person of Jesus Christ?
2. Have you ever applied the truths of Romans 12:1 – 2 to your life? How has this affected the way you live on a daily basis?
3. Have you ever struggled over something you felt God

calling you to do? What did you decide and how did your decision make you feel?

4. Who are your role models? How do his/her examples affect the way you live?

5. Describe your idea of what "full time Christian ministry" looks like.

6. To whom do you look to meet the needs you see: yourself? Others? God?

7. Explain the concept of Biblical boundaries in your own words.

8. Give an example from the Bible of someone who did or did not understand his or her boundaries.

Chapter Two – Accepted Before the First Miracle

1. What do you think is more important to God, who you are or what you do for Him? How does your answer affect the way you spend your time?

2. Are you a doer, an overachiever, or a perfectionist? If so, what do you think drives you to live that way?

3. Are you more comfortable watching others from the sidelines, or do you like to be in the middle of the game? Do you think this carries over into your spiritual life? How?

4. For further study about God's sovereignty over salvation, consider the following passages: Ephesians 1:3 – 2:10; Romans 8

5. Read Psalm 23 and discuss the insights you see related to boundaries.

6. Are you more concerned about pleasing God or pleasing others? How is your answer reflected in your daily decisions: what to wear, how to spend money, what to listen to, watch, etc.?

7. What are some practical ways to follow Jesus' example and demonstrate true humility? (Refer to Philippians 2:5 – 9)

Chapter Three – How to Identify Your Life Calling
1. What is God's ultimate goal for His children?
2. What is the believer's ultimate purpose for living?
3. What should be every believer's goal in life?
4. What is the "life calling" of the believer?
5. Define the "life work" of a believer.
6. Have you ever asked God to show you His calling on your life? If not, why not? If yes, what and how did He answer you?
7. Do you trust God to direct your life? Why or why not?
8. Make a list of three general commands in Scripture and put them somewhere you will see them frequently (bathroom mirror, computer screensaver, top of dresser, dashboard of car, etc.). Begin to follow these commands as you trust and pray for direction. Keep a journal of what happens as you walk in obedience.
9. Begin to keep a list of special verses you think may pertain to your life calling. After each one, write out how it applies to your calling. What themes do you see emerging?
10. Make a list of the important things in your life: family, work, hobbies, interests, relationships, etc. How do these line up with your verses and themes?

Chapter Four – Proper Priorities Produce Peace
1. Do you have a regular devotional life? Why or why not?
2. Is your relationship with God based on your personal knowledge of Him, what others have taught or modeled for you, or both? Explain your answer.
3. Are your quiet times a ritual or a delight? What steps can you take to make them consistently delightful?
4. Have you ever had to wait on God's timing for some-

thing? What did you learn from the experience?

5. Read Genesis 15:1 – 6, 16:1 – 12, 17:15 – 21, and 21:1 – 13. What are the consequences of not waiting for God's timing in this situation?

6. What does the word "rest" make you think of? Do you make time for rest a priority? Why or why not?

7. How can you determine the proper balance between work and rest for yourself?

Devotionals that have particularly encouraged me include the following:

1. <u>A Place of Quiet Rest</u>, Nancy Leigh DeMoss
2. <u>Spiritual Disciplines for the Christian Life</u>, Donald S. Whitney
3. <u>The Complete Works of E.M. Bounds on Prayer</u>
4. <u>Come Away My Beloved</u>, Frances J. Roberts
5. <u>My Utmost for His Highest</u>, Oswald Chambers

Chapter Five – Putting Prayer in its Proper Place – First

1. Discuss the implications of Richard Burr's statement, "One's spiritual life will never rise above the practice of one's private prayer life."

2. What are some ways to "listen" for God's voice in our praying?

3. About what kinds of things should we pray?

4. Why was prayer so important to Christ? Why should it be important to us?

5. What can we learn from the life of Christ about the proper balance between employing prayer and taking other actions to meet needs?

6. What are some practical ways to make prayer a priority in your daily routine, not just during devotions, but also throughout the day?

7. Discuss the implications of the author's statement, "When I act before praying, I live like an atheist."

8. With which hindrance to prayer do you struggle the most: self-sufficiency, impatience, or bitterness? What steps can you take to overcome this sin?
9. How is repentance a gift?
10. If you were to rate your level of trust in God on a scale from 1 – 10, with 1 being little trust and 10 being complete trust, where would you rate yourself? What steps can you take to build trust in God?

Chapter Six – Using Scripture to Pray Effectively
1. What is the value of learning to pray Scripture?
2. What passages of Scripture do you pray regularly? If none, make a list of three passages to begin praying on a regular basis. Write the verses on index cards and keep them handy so you can review them frequently.
3. Why do you think Christians neglect to "pray on" the armor of God listed in Ephesians 6?
4. Why is it important for a Christian to be a person who influences others for good?
5. Discuss your group's current prayer requests then use Paul's "power prayers" as a basis for lifting these requests to God as a group.
6. How is learning to pray Scripture a way of obeying Christ's command to seek God's kingdom and righteousness first? (See Matthew 6:33)

Chapter Seven – The Beauty of Discipleship: A Laser versus a Floodlight
1. Who has discipled you in your Christian life?
2. Have you ever discipled someone? How did you go about it? What did you learn from the experience?
3. What are some practical steps you can take to establish healthy emotional boundaries? Why are these necessary?
4. What does it mean to set realistic expectations of

others?
5. Draw your own "Circle of Concern" and "Circle of Influence." Can you identify any ways in which you have violated your boundaries by not limiting detours? What can you do to better focus on your "Circle of Influence?"
6. Have you ever overextended yourself? What motivated you to do that? How can you avoid that in the future?
7. Why is discipleship so important?

Chapter Eight – Following the Leader
Principles of Leadership:
- Choose your answers carefully.
- Understand and accept that leadership is lonely.
- Learn to model humility.
- Graciously accept praise when appropriate.
- Be firm when necessary.
- Learn to reason dispassionately.
- Discern between the proud and the humble.
- Give of your time.
- Be willing to share the spotlight.
- Envision great things for those you lead.
- Stay under authority.

1. Do you feel intimidated by the thought of being a leader? Why or why not?
2. Who has God called you to lead? Are you leading them in a positive way?
3. Identify the areas of leadership in which you are most comfortable.
4. Choose one area to focus on improving.
5. Purpose to pray through the list of principles on a regular basis, asking God to build these into your life.

Chapter Nine – Making the Most of Inevitable Opposition

1. What are three ways Jesus models or explains for handling opposition from those we know?
2. Think of a time when you faced "opposition" from a friend. How did you respond?
3. Briefly describe Biblical guidelines for handling opposition from the world.
4. Have you ever faced personal opposition from someone or some group outside your acquaintance? How did that make you feel? What did you learn from the experience?
5. What are some man-made traditions in your church or group of Christian friends? Based on the example and words of Christ, how should you handle these? Consider Romans 14 for further study and discussion.
6. How does the sovereignty of God affect the growth and understanding of believers?
7. How does God illustrate for us the ways to deal with opposition?

Chapter Ten – Infirmity: Friend or Fear?

1. What differences have you found between spiritual, emotional, and physical demands in your life? How do each of these affect your physical strength, emotional outlook and spiritual relationship with God?
2. Are you willing to share your struggles with God and others? Why or why not?
3. Discuss John Piper's definition of the "debtor's ethic." Can you relate to this? If so, how?
4. How can physical boundaries become blessings?
5. In what ways does faith affect physical healing?
6. Have you ever been angry with God? Consider following the steps to emotional healing outlined in this chapter and praying through those feelings.

7. Think about a difficult situation in your life. In what ways could God be using this to draw you to Himself and conform you to the image of Christ?

Chapter Eleven – The Blessing of Boundaries

1. Why does God give us boundaries?
2. How does living within our boundaries glorify God?
3. Is ministry a job or a way of life? Explain your answer.
4. What is the difference between accepting the reality of the "inevitables" in life and doing nothing to extend the kingdom of God?
5. Explain the difference between passive and active obedience to the commands of Christ.
6. Why is daily faithfulness so important?
7. What are some of the emotional boundaries God gives us in Scripture?
8. What is the fruit of a life committed to discovering the blessing within boundaries?

Selected Bibliography

Balch, Phyllis A, CNC and Balch, James F., M.D., <u>Prescription for Nutritional Healing</u>, 3rd Edition, Avery, New York, 2000

Barnhart, Clarence L. (editor), <u>The Thorndike Barnhart Comprehensive Desk Dictionary</u>, Doubleday and Company, Inc., Garden City, New York, 1954

Berkhof, L., <u>Systematic Theology</u>, 3rd edition, WM. B. Eerdmans Publishing Company, Grand Rapids, MI 1946

Bounds, E.M., <u>The Complete Works of E.M. Bounds on Prayer</u>, Baker Book House, Grand Rapids, Michigan, 1990

Burr, Richard A., <u>Developing Your Secret Closet of Prayer</u>, Christian Publications, Camp Hill, Pennsylvania, 1998

Hanley, Jesse Lynn, M.D. and Deville, Nancy, <u>Tired of Being Tired</u>, G.P. Putnam's Sons, New York, 2001

<u>Hymns for the Living Church</u>, Hope Publishing Company, Carol Stream, Illinois, 1974

James, Carolyn Custis, <u>When Life and Beliefs Collide, How Knowing God Makes a Difference</u>, Zondervan Publishing House, Grand Rapids, MI, 2001

Murray, John, <u>Behind a Frowning Providence</u>, The Banner of Truth Trust, Carlisle, PA, 1990

Packer, J.I., <u>God's Words: Studies of Key Bible Themes</u>, Baker Book House, Grand Rapids, MI, 1981

Piper, John, <u>Desiring God</u>, Multnomah Publishers, Inc. Sisters, Oregon, 1996

Piper, John, <u>Future Grace</u>, Multnomah Publishers, Inc. Sisters, Oregon, 1995

Powlison, David, <u>Power Encounters: Reclaiming Spiritual Warfare</u>, Baker Books, Grand Rapids, MI, 1995

Sahelian, Ray, M.D. "Inner Peace: Finding Freedom from Stress and Anxiety," *healthsmart today*, Spring 2002

<u>The Westminster Confession of Faith</u>, Committee for Christian Education and Publications, reprinted in 1990

Welch, Edward T., <u>Addictions, A Banquet in the Grave: Finding Hope in the Power of the Gospel</u>, P&R Publishing, Phillipsburg, NJ, 2001

Welch, Edward T. <u>When People Are Big and God Is Small</u>, P&R Publishing, Phillipsburg, NJ, 1997

Printed in the United States
29148LVS00004B/85-117